Beyond the Chronicles

Beyond the Chronicles

'Recovering' Histories of the Institutions and Families

[Persian Documents in India, 17th-19th C.]

Saiyid Zaheer Husain Jafri

GYAN

ISBN: 978-81-212-2017-0

Published, 2021

Published by

Gyan Publishing House
5, Ansari Road
Daryaganj, New Delhi-110002
Phone: 011-47034999, 9811692060
www.gyanbooks.com
E-mail: books@gyanbooks.com

To

Professor Irfan Habib Saheb

My Teacher, Supervisor, Guide & Mentor

Contents

Acknowledgements

The chapters included in the volume have resulted during the initial decades of my research and teaching career [between the years 1979-97]. I respectfully acknowledge my teacher, Prof Irfan Habib, (now Professor Emiretus at Aligarh Muslim University) to have taught me the basic nuances for using the archival records. It was under his guidance that I learned to cull the researchable material from the documents and under his guidance I practiced to learn the *shikasta* script. I owe so much to him that perhaps I cannot express it adequetly in words. I shall ever remain grateful for his many acts of kindness.

I express my gratitude to my teachers especially to Prof Shireen Moosvi, Late Prof M.Athar Ali, Late Prof Iqbal Husain, Prof Ishtiyaq Ahmad Zilli and Prof. Afzal Husain for support, advice and whatever help I needed in understanding the material which I am presenting in this volume.

I wish to place on record my gratitude to my cousin late Shah Mohammad Hameed Ata 'Hassan' [d. 2005] for sharing documents on our family history from the Nawabi era which were in his personal collection, some of them are reproduced in the appendix. It was but for him that I would not have been able to access these documents from anywhere.

My friends Dr. Zakir Husain [recently retired as Deputy Director, Oriental records, National Archives of India, New Delhi], Mr Saiyid Aslam Ali and Faizan Ahmad Islahi for their help while working at the correction of acquired documents in Oriental Records division of National Archive of Indian.

I want to put on record that the documents included here in the appendix were very kindly transcribed in the fair hand by Prof Ishtiyaq Ahmad Zilli and Mr Saiyid Aslam Ali. It was Zilli Saheb who carefully transcribed the two *farmans* of Aurangzeb belonging to my family from the notes of which Prof Irfan Habib has taken of the *farman* before they were destroyed in an unfortunate incident of arson of my belonging at my hostel room of Aligarh Muslim University Campus on 13th May 1981. The remaining other documents included here were transcribed by Mr Saiyid Aslam Ali, my friend who was working for his PhD thesis in Aligarh during that period.

My students have always been a source of strength for me. I have been teaching an optional paper on 'Archives: Epigraphy and Numismatics during Medieval India' to the successive batches of MA Final students at North Campus, Delhi University and some of the arguments I have given in the introduction has resulted from my interaction with my inquisitive students. Their comments and queries have made me to finetune some of my unorganized thoughts. At the final stage of preparation of the manuscript, I received help from my student Dr Heena Ansari [now a colleague in the Department of History], Ms Yusra Farooqui and Dr. Syed Shahid Ashraf.

Once again, I take the opportunity to express my gratitude to my wife, Mrs. Tayyaba Jafri and to my sons Saiyid Naseer Jafri (Tariq), Saiyid Ashraf Jafri (Abbas) and daughter Haleema Sadia Jafri for being considerate, in allowing me to work in the Department up to the late hours.

Needless to say that I am most grateful to Garg Saheb, the proprietor of Gyan Books, for undertaking this project during the time of unfortunate pandemic.

4th Zilhijj AH 1442/15th July 2021

Saiyid Zaheer Husain Jafri
Department of History
University of Delhi

Previous Publication Details

Chapter 1: 'A Farman of Akbar [1558] from the period of the Regency', in *Akbar and His India*, ed., Irfan Habib, 1997, OUP Delhi, pp. 266-269.

Chapter 2: 'Theologians and Revenue Grantees in Sarkar Sambhal: Facets of Local Administration under Akbar', Seminar: *Akbar and His Age*, Centre of Advanced Study in History, Aligarh Muslim University, Aligarh, 9-11 October, 1992.

Chapter 3: 'Administration of *Jagirs* in Awadh during 17th Century', *UP Historical Review,* Vol. 3, Allahabad, 1983, pp. 57-63.

Chapter 4: 'Mughal Relations with Portuguese Administration in Goa 1700-1701: Evidence of Persian Records in Lisbon Archives', *Proceeding of Indian History Congress* [Goa Session], 1987, pp. 302-311.

Chapter 5: 'The Sarkar Qanungo: 16th-17th Century Documents, *PIHC* [Amritsar Session], 1985, pp. 253-264.

Chapter 6: 'Side Lights on Administrative Structure and Agrarian Relations in Awadh- A Study of Laharpur Documents [16th-18th century]', Seminar on *Sources of Socio-Economic History of North India,* Department of Meideval and Modern Indian History, University of Allahabad, Feb-March, 1985.

Chapter 7: Rural Bureaucracy in Cooch Bihar and Assam under the Mughals: Archival Evidence, *PIHC* [Dharwar Session], 1988, pp. 277-286.

Chapter 8: 'Tension and Conflict in the Agrarian Society of Awadh: A Study of the Revenue Grantees', *PIHC*, 1990 [Calcutta Session], pp. 354-361.

Chapter 9: 'Two *Madad-e Ma'ash Farmans* of Aurangzeb from Awadh', *PIHC* [Waltair Session], 1979, pp. 302-314.

Chapter 10: 'Landed Properties of a Sufi Establishment-Calendar of 17th and 18th century Documents from Salon in Awadh', *PIHC*, 47 Session, Srinagar, 1986, pp. 417-431.

Documents and Map

Documents from Parganas Sambhal, Baiswara, Cooch Behar and Thana Rangamati

Documents from Khanqah-i-Karimia Pargana Salon

Map

A Testimonial of Professor Irfan Habib

ALIGARH HISTORIANS SOCIETY
Regd.No.Ag-22857

AHS

IRFAN HABIB
Professor of History (rtd.)
PRESIDENT

Centre of Advanced Study
Department of History
Aligarh Muslim University
Aligarh-202002. India

Website
http://members.tripod.com/ahsaligarh

It gives me great pleasure to write these words in commendation of Dr S. Zaheer Husain Jafri, partly for bearing with my eccentricities when I was his Supervisor for his Ph.D. thesis. Dr Jafri comes from a family of sufis of an important shrine at Salon; and his interest in History possibly derived from documents in possession of his family going back to the reign of Aurangzeb.

Dr Jafri studied at the AMU for his B.A. and M.A. degrees, and in both courses attended my lectures in papers on Modern India and Economic History of Mughal India. He passed his M.A. in the First Division. While pursuing research on the Agrarian History of Awadh from the 16th Century to the British Annexation of Awadh (1856), he made good use of his knowledge of Persian. He studied at the Allahabad Record Office, which has a massive collection of original Persian documents from the 16th century. I believe he is one of the very few scholars who have worked so intensively on this material. He mastered

Telephone: (Deptt.) 0571-2705792 (Res.) 0571-2702620. Telefax:2701539 E-mail:ahs@ndf.vsnl.net.in the shikasta or cursive Mughal script, and showed considerable ingenuity in interpreting the documents. Dr Jafri writes and speaks English fluently, and his thesis was a well-written piece.

I was sorry that our Department lost him, in 1986 to the Delhi University. Since then, I have read several papers by him dealing with both the history of Awadh and with archival materials. I consider his book *Studies in the Anatomy of Transformation*, 1998, an important contribution to the study of the conditions of 19th-century Awadh. I also look forward to the publication of his thesis.

I am sure Dr Jafri has a bright career further ahead of him, and we can expect significant contributions to the study of medieval Indian history from him.

Irfan Habib

3 October 2004

Introduction

I

Migrants, Knowledge, State and Society

'The dissemination of knowledge in the Islamic East' was mainly organized by the individuals; it was the high academic status and stature of the Sheikh, based on his familial connections that attracted the seekers of knowledge around him. These 'circles' around the person of the Sheikh ultimately emerged as the centers of learning. The State and even the civil society took care of their needs and provided financial resources for meeting out their expenses. That is how the knowledge and education grew in the Muslim societies. The State sponsored institutions of education were also there but change of regime and the lack of official patronage often led to their demise. We hear of the *Madrasas* established by Nizam ul Mulk Tusi, the famous Saljuq prime minister, Sultan Firoz Shah Tughlaq and Mughal emperor Shahjahan, but these State sponsored ventures have not survived beyond few generations. While the institutions around individuals with the full backing of the civil society continued and often multiplied almost uninterrupted. Hence, there is a close connection between the centers for the dissemination of knowledge and creation of the numerous *Awqaf* in the Muslim Societies.

The institution of the *Waqf* emerged as the most crucial social institution throughout the Islamic East. The creation of innumerable endowments for the upkeep of the three holiest *Masjids* of Islam (the holy *Ka'aba*; Prophet's Mosque at the holy city of Medina and al-*Aqsa* mosque at Jerusalem) the and for upkeep of the holy shrines of Najaf, Karbala and Mashhad are in fact so numerous that even one would lose its actual count. Apart from these holiest religious places, there are thousands and thousands of institutions which have enjoyed endowments in the past millennium. The holders and keepers of these revenue free grants have always in the then contemporaneous world enjoyed respect; they also discharged their obligations towards society by promoting knowledge, disseminating education and discharging of other social obligations. Recently some studies on *waqf* have been undertaken to highlight this aspect in a remarkable manner. Professor R.D. MacChesney's *Waqf in Central Asia: Four Hundred years in the History of a Muslim Shrine, 1480-1889* [Princeton, 1991]; Professor Toru Miura's, *"Dynamism in the Urban Society of Damascus, The Salihiyya Quarter from the Twelfth to the Twentieth Centuries* [Brill, 2015], and her edited volume, *Comparative Study of the Waqf from the East; Dynamism of Norm and Practices in Religious and Familial Donations* [Tokyo, 2018] are the important and detailed studies of the subject in the recent decades. In fact, these studies have opened up window for undertaking the institutional histories of the *Waqf* in other parts in the Islamic East. A series of the *waqf* conferences are being organized at the various Universities to study the subject historically. The legal and the social implications of the subject are the important aspects which are highlighted in these conferences. Hopefully, in the coming years more studies on the subject are likely to come up.

The ecclesiastical institutions and families connected with these centers and enjoying revenue-free grants were to preserve the documents relating to their rights as subsequent confirmation depended on the evidence in support of their fiscal claims. *The Historical Documents Purchase Committee* and the *Indian Historical Records Commission* made efforts to acquire these collections from the inmates of these institutions and the families enjoying the ecclesiastical offices like the *qazis* and others. However, a large number of documents still remain with the families connected with the mystic and temple establishments. Some of such collections keep on surfacing in the acquisitions of archives and museums.

Often these grants are described as charitable grants. However, none of the official documents, chronicles and administrative manuals has ever used the words/expressions, especially meant to describe/convey the sense for charity or for the charitable uses while making such grants. The terms which are used to describe the charity in the *fiqh* and other Islamic literature like *sadqah*, *khairat*, *fitrah*, or *zakat* have never been employed either in the Chronicles or in the Archival papers to describe the *madad-i ma'ash* grants. Thus, to place *madad-i ma'ash* under the category of 'charity' is inappropriate. Instead, common neutral terms like *Suyurghal*, *a'imma* and *madad-i ma'ash* or *inam* and in the later period *ma'afi* is invariably used to describe these grants in the official papers of Mughal and Nawabi periods. Such nomenclature is used invariably irrespective of the religious affiliation of the recipient unlike our modern Indian State which makes a distinction not only on the basis of religious affiliation but also on the basis of sectarian affiliations. Therefore, we have Shia/Sunni waqf board, Devottar and Brahmottar grants in the modern times.[1]

However, irrespective of the 'nature' of the grants, the recipients themselves thought these grants as something held on loan [*ariyat*] and consider themselves simply as the trustee [*muttawalli*] and not the owner [*malik*] of these grants. During the classical period of Mughal Empire, it is worth to recall some evidence from the documents we have included in the present volume itself. The Salon family became the recipient of the first imperial grant only in AD 1676, where the *Farman* describes the grant in a highly respectful manner. It uses the expression *nazr-e khadiman-e haqaiq wa agah* [an offering for the servants of the one who knows the mystic truths]. The second imperial grant came in succession where young son of the mystic was named as the recipient in AD1679. Within three decades another imperial *farman* of Mughal Emperor Bahadur Shah I of 1708 officially recognizes:

> ……the grantee with a large number of mendicants is engaged in propagating the tenets of *sharia* and *tariqat* in the area and that in some of these villages he has established mosque, *musafirkhana* and, in the barren land has caused habitations to come up and has named after his sons.

Perhaps, such recognition of the role this migrant family established at Salon was playing in the area has resulted into numerous subsequent imperial grants. It also needs to point out that invariably all the imperial grants recognize the alienation of land rights in favor of the family members of the mystic by the local landed magnets, chieftains and zamindars. The grantees were already 'possessing' the lands and villages which were now conferred on them by the imperial decrees so that the future jagirdars and officials may not create problems for the family.

By the time of beginning of Nawabi rule in Awadh from 1722 onwards, the *khanqah* of Salon emerged as an unique institution in the province; the grants remained continued more or less and this *khanqah* seems to have been the largest of its kind in the southern Awadh. Its annual income was estimated by Donald Butler in 1836 at Rs. 30,000 utilized in 'entertaining '*bairagis*' and '*fakirs*' without any distinction of religion': 'a large number of visitors flocked to the *khanaqah* and at times there could even be about a hundred mendicants staying at the *musafirkhana*. These were attended to and looked after by the *sajjadanashin* of the *khanaqah,* whose reputation was such that any new '*Chakladar* appointed in the *Nizamat* of Salon promptly paid a visit and offered a few hundred rupees as *nazr'*.'[2] In the context of the plurality and composite culture Butler also says that 'the famed Maulvi [Saiyid Ahmad of Rae Bareli] could not gain much in Salon, as he was told by the zamindars and the miyan [local title for sajjadanashin] that for them relieving and aiding the poor, the lame and the blind was more pious than indulging in the holy war.' They also told him clearly that they intend to follow the example of the forefather 'in carrying tazias [tinsel shrines] at the *Muharram*.' Perhaps, the presence of Khanqah in midst of the Rajput population helped in creating conditions which made conditions conducive for a situation which has been described by Butler as:

> 'The religious excitability of the Muslims of Oudh seems to range lower than that of their co-religionists in Rohilkhand in the Haidarabad states, or even in Bengal.'[3]

Col. W H Sleeman, the famous and even controversial British Resident at Nawabi Court of Awadh, while undertaking a tour in the kingdom of Oudh [December 1849- February 1850] refers to this establishment as the prime mystic institution of the kingdom. Shah Panah Ata, the then *sajidanashin* of the *khanqah,* was looked upon with great reverence by both Muslims and Hindus due to the sanctity of his ancestors and of the institution. He is said to have never left the *khanaqah*: 'he remained there to receive the homage and distribute the needy and the travelers belonging to all religions.' Sleeman estimated the annual income from the grant held by him in AD 1850 at about Rs. 25,000. In addition to this income, several local officials and princes from places as distant as Bhopal, Sironj, and Rewa had made substantial offerings. Taking all these into account, the actual income of the establishment was calculated to have been about Rs. 50,000 a year.[4]

Relations of the establishment with the British were cordial, to begin with. Complimentary letters were sent to Shah Panah Ata by the Governor-General of India, and the Lieutenant Governors of the North-west provinces. When Colonel W.H.

Sleeman was passing through the district of Salon, Shah Panah Ata sent him 'letters of compliments and welcome with a present of tame antelope, some fruits and sugar'. This goodwill gesture was reciprocated by Sleeman who records that 'his (the Shaikh's) character is held in high esteem by all classes of people, of whatever creed, caste or grade'. In spite of this cordiality with East India Company and Nawabi regime, when the joint action by the Company's and Nawab's forces led to the unfortunate incident of the martyrdom of Maulvi Saiyid Amir Ali, a *pirzada* of Amethi and 300 companions at Bhilsar crossing near Rudauli on 7th November 1855. While Maulvi Amir Ali has mobilized the people for reconstructing the destroyed mosque at Hanumangarhi, Ayodhya by the *bairagis*. The *sajjadanashin* Shah Panah Ata felt tormented and condemned the Nawabi regime for its inaction, complicity and mischief. He described maulvi Amir Ali as a *shahid* and even compared *shahid* and composed numerous chronograms praising him, his companions and thoroughly condemning Nawab Wajid Ali Shah.[5]

The condemnation of the Nawabi regime after the martyrdom of Amir Ali did not prevent Shah Panah Ata to condemn the unjustified act of East India Company i.e., annexation of Oudh soon after Hanumangarhi incident i.e., in Feb. 1856 with deep anguish. Shah Panah Ata thoroughly condemned the high handedness of British in quite unambiguous terms and expressed his feelings saying: *Zulm-i Wajid beh ze adl-i Company* (the [so-called] oppression by Wajid Ali Shah was better than the 'justice' of Company').[6]

Such open expression of anti-British sentiments led to the confiscation of properties of *Sajjada nashin* between annexation of Awadh to the mutiny, but the punitive move had to be restored due to the strong social acceptability and prestige the institution held among Hindus and Muslims. This was in spite of very strong opposition by the then Deputy Commissioner recommending the confiscation of the grant due to the support *khanqah* gave to the rebels of 1857. His opinion is worth quoting:

> The incumbent of these rent-free grants rendered and the British government no assistance during the rebellion [...] these 22 villages be granted in perpetuity on condition of (a) the offering of a *nazrana* [i.e succession duty] of ₹ 28,000/- by the grantee on the receipt of the Governor General's farman; (b) the payment of ₹ 28,000/- one year's rental by each of the successors [...] As this is a trust fund, the government should reserve to itself the power of interfering in the expenditure, should it think proper to do so?[7]

Major Barrow had made an initial inquiry into the credential of the grantee, but none of the files and papers pertaining to this inquiry are available. These must have been burnt during the revolt of 1857. A second enquiry was conducted in the 1860s by W.C. Wood (then deputy commissioner of Prapatgarh), carrying the history of landed properties accruing to the family since the period of Aurangzeb, the details of buildings belonging to the institution and maintained out of the *waqf* fund, and incomes and heads on which the expenditures were incurred. A distinction between the personal expenses of *sajjada nashin* (Which never exceeded 1/5th of the total income) and of the institution was made. On the basis of this report and on behalf of Lord Canning, a *sanad* was issued on 26th Sep 1862, recognizing the allodial rights of Shah Husain Ata [the then *sajjadanashin*] over 22 villages of his grant. However, now the grant was made a conditional one: it was to continue only as long as the income was devoted to the maintenance of the *Khanqah*, buildings, tomb, mosque, and the running of a school of 'Muhammadan Education' and the continuance of the 'charities' [which were already done by the family and which has been detailed in W.C.Wood's dispatch].

The *sanad* is quoted in full to illustrate few points:

> It having been established after due enquiry that Shah Husain Ata held under-mentioned land in *tehsil Salon, zila* Pratapgarh in rent-free tenure under the former government; the Chief Commissioner under the authority of the Governor-General-in-Council is pleased to maintain the tenure so long as the grantees perform their duties and keep the buildings and school according to the terms of the grant on the following conditions:
>
> 1. That he shall have surrendered all *Sanad*, deeds, and documents relating to the tenure in question
> 2. That he and his successors shall strictly perform all the duties of landholders in matters of police and any military or political service that may be required of them by the authorities
> 3. That they shall never fall under the just suspicion of favoring in any way the designs of the enemies of the British government and
> 4. If anyone of these conditions is broken by the present incumbent or any of his successors, the tenure will be immediately resumed.

It might look ironical but this *Sanad* granted by the British government under the spell of great uprising of 1857 though recognizes the superior rights of grantee but it totally alters the tone and tenure of the grant. The ancestors of this Migrant family of the Sufis and Scholars might have been very revered personalities and scholarly figures for the earlier regimes but now 'they are assigned police, military, and political duties.' Their status is now sought to be reduced, if not to the level of 'collaborators' then certainly to that of 'informers'. Such humiliating stipulations do not leave much to the imagination by way of understanding how these institutions would have struggled to exist under the changed circumstances.

While examining the evidence from Bengal Presidency and the impact of infamous *Inam* Commission, [1828-46] which practically destroyed the Muslim *Ashrafia* of Bengal, Bihar, Orrisa and Assam during the period and has reduced the centers of Indo-Islamic learning prior to 1857. Almost the same fate awaited the fortunes of Indo-Islamic learning and the migrant families of scholars and Sufis in Awadh after 1857. Thus, the region which was nostalgically referred to by Mughal Emperor Shahjahan during the hay-day of Mughal ruler as *Purab Shiraz-e Hind mamlakat-e ma ast* was reduced to such a level that the families which carried forward the tradition of learning to the highest level were now thoroughly marginalized and excluded. This disastrous impact not only ruined the institutions and the families associated with these centers: it had another far-reaching impact the rise of the radical tendencies among the masses. At the initial stages, we noticed that the *Fara'izi* and Wahabi movements derived their main strength and support base from the regions where the colonial administration marginalized the traditional elite and practically destroyed the earlier institutions of learning.[8]

Thus, it is more than obvious that the migrant families who were the recipients of the land free grants from the State and other financial favors from the local landed elite and overlords in the form of land and cash grants were making use of their income in establishing the institutions, erecting the buildings for the public welfare, disseminating the knowledge and last but not the least establishing a free kitchen to feed the mendicants irrespective of their religious affiliations. Hence, the 'charitable use' of the income derived from the revenue free grants was done by the recipients themselves, rather than they were the recipients of the 'charitable grants'.

II

Records from the Ecclesiastical Families and the understanding of Chancellery Practices

The mystic and temple families were more often involved in long drawn litigation and for an adjudication of their rights they used to file the Mughal documents in support of their claims. Some of such documents have found their way in the files at the record rooms of the District Courts and the Board of Revenue Library. Apart from providing history of the individual families connected with the mystic and temple establishments, these files talk much about the British policy towards the *ma' afidars* after 1857, and multiplicity of land rights acquired by *ma'afi* holders. Between the Summary Settlement and the First Regular Settlement *(bandobast-i awwal)*, British officers compiled exhaustive reports examining the claims of the *ma' afidars* and the nature of their grants at the time of the annexation of Awadh in February 1856. The objects of such enquiries were limited to the terms at which new *Sanads* were to be granted. The meticulously prepared *wajib-ul arz* of each village and *rawaje a'am* of each *pargana* recorded the customary laws of the then landowning classes regarding a wide range of matters. Such documents are extremely valuable for giving us a peep into the Agrarian society of Awadh during the earlier periods as well.

In the world of 'spirituality' the *sufi* institutions have 'created' records having a bearing on the hierarchy in the 'world of spirituality'. The deeds of initiation into discipleship and nomination of successors like *shajra, khilafatnamah,* and *misali khilafat wa janashini* often used to spell out the *Sufi* customs and traditions. Since the question of nomination was closely linked to the control of the landed property attached to the institutions by way of *madad-i-ma'ash,* such visualizations ultimately resulted in the change of the character of the grant. The institution of *waqf* was also created in such establishments even when the grants were initially made for the personal expenses.

Records of this kind are also to be found scattered in the files of the Board of Revenue (records upto AD 1890 have now been transferred to UP State Archives, Lucknow) and in files of judicial proceedings. Many are, of course, still in private hands.

Indian sub-continent happened to be a major melting pot for the fusion of Islamic culture. The 'migrant literary and theological elite' arriving from the various Central Asian cities and towns have brought the elements of 'Islamic Culture' with them. Due to their presence in the city of Delhi and various parts of the Indian sub-continent, a number of *maktab* and *madrasa* were established in these towns and other centers to cater the need of emerging Muslim population. Shaikh Rizqullah Mushtaqi, while writing about the reign of Sultan Sikandar Lodi, very specifically says that:

> "In each town and region, where the forces of Islam have gained an upper hand and have become popular, *masajid, jam'at khana* and *khanqah* were established and the capable people were appointed in the *maktabs and* the *madrasa* as the *mu'allim* and *muddarris*. In these institutions, the *umra'* and their sons and the sons of the soldiers acquired knowledge and busied themselves in the prayer and meditations. Those who could afford discharged their duties in the way of God (by offering monetary support). The institution so established trained the inmates for the emerging needs of the administration and the bureaucracy, the *Qazis* (judicial officers), the expert accountants, scribes and other state functionaries were the products of these institutions"[9]

The strong intellectual and academic tradition of the region became quite proverbial and people nostalgically recalled it even after its heydays were over. Ghulam 'Ali Azad Bilgrami (d. 1761), while paying glowing tribute to the cultural life in the Upper Gangetic Valley, has said that "this region since the olden days (*qadim-ul ayyam*) has been the cradle of knowledge and center for the scholars (*ma'adan-e 'Ilm wa maskan-e 'Ulema*)". According to him the Mughal *suba* of Awadh and Allahabad enjoyed special status as compared to other provinces of the empire in the sphere of intellectual activities. There were innumerable intellectual centers and numerous scholars, that these two *suba* had 'a major settlement of Muslim intellectual elite (*shurufa wa nujaba'*] at every 5 to 10 *kroh'*. They had been well-provided by the earlier *salatin* with cash and *madad e ma'ash* grants.

This had facilitated the establishment of mosques, *madrasas,* and *khanqahs* all over the province, where the teachers of all disciplines were busy in the dissemination of knowledge. The students trained at these institutions went to other parts of the country and established and strengthened this intellectual tradition further. It is important to note that Azad Bilgrami specifically says that the well- provided section of the society took extra care of the requirements of these scholars and considered serving them an act of great benefit (*sa 'adat-e 'uzma*) for themselves.[10]

It might look ironical that while the records of the Mughal State have rarely survived, the family papers of the grantees and institutions, who sought the legitimacy from the Mughal State, have somehow survived. Based on this documentation it has been possible for the students of Mughal History to work out the details of the structure of the society, agrarian relations, the rural overlords and their relationship with the migrant elite, the institutional histories of numerous *Awqafs*. Some of these institutions have survived till the modern times and have also been engaged in the litigations, therefore, their records from the 16th century onwards are available in the numerous files at the board of revenue and various Courts of Law. Most of the records are in *shikasta* style of writing which requires some expertise in decipherment. However, the scholars have been able to use the data in the most imaginative manner.

Besides the pioneer studies in the early 20th century like J.J Modi's *Parsies at the Court of Akbar: Dastur Meharji Rana,* Bombay, 1903 and K.M Jhaveri's, *The Imperial Farmans {AD.1577-85} Granted to the Ancestors of Tikayat Maharaj,* Bombay 1928, numerous seminal studies have been published on the subject in the later half of the 20th century, especially the works of Momin Mohiuddin, S.A.I Tirmizi, Yusuf Husain Khan, J.S Grewal, B.N Goswami and last but not the least Prof. Irfan Habib have added to our knowledge on the institutional and social history of the Mughal times. The most recent discovery by late Prof Tarapad Mukherjee of the *Vrindavan-Mathura* documents has almost altered our understanding of Mughal State and the temples of Mathura region.

The chancellery practices and the forms of writing official and semi-official documents have evolved during pre-colonial times in a gradual manner, so much so that during the reign of Mughal emperor Akbar and especially after the initial decades of his reign, these practices have taken a definite form. The *insha* writers and their numerous collections [*munsha'at*] have almost settled the official and semi-official forms of writing and documentation. The professional class of the *munshis* enjoyed the patronage of every section of society for their expertise in drafting the petitions and letters. Unlike the official historians and histories which often employed adjectives and a text full with verbosity and exaggerations, the epistolary and especially the language employed in the official papers was generally simple, direct and very 'business' like. There were little need and scope for the adjectives and panegyrics. Also, the records from the chancellery department were closer to the actual measures: as they talk more about the actual measure to be adopted, they describe the details of all the official procedure, resulting into the passage of the actual measure/order. This was quite unlike of the information in the chronicles and the contemporary texts which generally mentions about some of these administrative measures only in passing and not providing the procedural details and other related complexities into those measures.

One finds that the early specimens survived from the time of Emperor Akbar imply the terms and nomenclatures for the offices/department as well as for the persons responsible for those departments as it existed during the previous administration. Therefore, we notice that in some of the early surviving records we encounter the term *jaygir/jaygirdaar* which was later on standardized as simple term *jagir/jagirdar.* Similarly, one notices the use of the term *suyurghal* for the revenue free grants in some surviving records of 16th century while in the later period we encounter the term *madad-e maash* as a common term for almost every revenue-free grant. This becomes especially interesting when we find this term occuring for every revenue-free grant: for the *Sufis*, for the holders of temple grant as well as those who are deserving of the imperial favors for their incapacity to earn for themselves. No distinction is made as far as the term is concerned for the recipient of the grant.

The recipient of these grants kept these official papers with care, as the renewal of their posting and the reconfirmation of every imperial favor invariably require the production of the earlier grant. Hence, every confirmatory order always had a recitation to the effect that the recipient has possessed some grant/office from the earlier times. Hence, the new administration was somehow obliged to confirm the earlier grants. This way, the documents were preserved by the families which enjoyed the *madad-e ma'ash* or some rural bureaucratic posting like the office of *qanungo* or *chadhurai* which was conferred on some families on a hereditary basis. These private records were kept by the descendants of the family of the recipient as their 'heritage'. Sometime these papers were produced during the colonial times in case of some family dispute or in the settlement of their claims during the enquiries by the Settlement officers. In cases of the civil litigation related to the adjudication of individual rights, these papers from pre-colonial times often provide a clinching evidence for the continuity of certain rights. Similarly , they were equally useful in deciding the family disputes.

The administrative documents, the papers of the revenue grantees and the papers related to the hereditary rights of village officials are of immense value for understanding the pre-colonial society in a better manner, for the chronicles, historical texts and other material seldom talk about these matters or provide hardly any clue about such people or institutions. Realizing the importance of the intrinsic value of such data Historical Documents Purchase Committee as well Indian Historical Records Commission made an effort to approach the individual, families and institutions who deposit, donate or sell these papers to the public institutions so that the students are able to study the material historically. Thus, the collections at Regional Record Offices, Allahabad, UP State Archives, Lucknow, National Archives of India, Department of Historical and Antiquarian Studies, Guwahati and last but not the least Telangana State Archives, Hyderabad emerged as the important repositories of such documents.

Series of catalogues, calendars of the documents and the actual facsimiles of the *farmans* and village papers with their transliteration as well translations were published from time to time. Yusuf Husain Khan's *Selected Documents of Shahjahan's Reign* [Hyderabad, 1950] set the high standards of such endeavors. Thereafter, Ziyauddin Shaqeb's *Mughal Imperial Farmans* [Hyderabad, 1977] was to be an equally commendable effort in this direction. SAI Tirmizi's *Edicts from*

Mughal Harem [Delhi, 1976] provided the documentary evidence for the crucial role of royal ladies in Mughal administration. The effort to bring out the Mughal imperial *farmans* and other equally important papers at numerous archives and record rooms continue to yield fresh material for the students of history. The publications from Lucknow, Bikaner and Sitamau archives are notable.

However, it needs to be highlighted that the above publications highlighted the importance of 'repositories' as holding the primary material at their disposal. They also highlighted the importance enjoyed by certain families like that of Tiket Maharaj or the Parsi physicians who were the recipient of Mughal imperial favors. Hence, the argument could have been made to understand the Mughal policy of ecclesiasticism and recognizing the individual merit of the grantees.

We notice a notable trend with the publication of a seminal article of Irfan Habib wherein he has used the information in the revenue documents to study the aspects of agrarian and economic history of a small locality from which these documents were acquired. The papers relating to Mughal parganas Bilgram and Shamsabad begin from the time of emperor Babar and coming up to the close of Aurangzeb's reign could be used to understand the aspects which are totally missing from the chronicles. This study proves to be a landmark attempt made as early as 1967.[11] Soon after B. N Goswami and J.S.Grewal came up with the splendid volume, *The Mughal and the Jogis of Jaghbhar: Some Madad-e M'ash and Other Documents* [Shimla, 1969] by using the Mughal imperial *Farmans*, they have studied this *nathpanthi* seat of *jogies* in the present day Gurdaspur district of Punjab. It was a documentary history of Shrine totally based on Mughal official records for about two hundred years. This study was the beginning of numerous other such works like *In the Bi-lanes of History* [Shimla] *The Batala Documents* [Shimla] and

M Azhar Ansari's explorations of the documents of *Jangambari math* at Varanasi published as *The Administrative Documents of Mughal Empire* [Delhi, 1981].

The data from these documents have been used most imaginatively by Professor Irfan Habib in his book *Braj Bhum in Mughal Times: The State, Peasants and Gosains'* (Delhi: Primus, 2020) which had open new avenues to understand the dynamics and the interdependence of religious and agrarian classes and their relationship with the State. Similarly, the recent publications of Mohammed Suleman Siddiqi, *Junaydi Sufis of the Deccan: Discovery of a Seventeenth Century Scroll* (Delhi: Primus, 2014); Iqbal Husain's *Studies in the Polity, Economy and Society of the Trans-Gangetic Valley, 15th-19th Centuries* (Delhi: Primus, 2013) and Zakir Husain's, *Medieval India: Studies in Polity, Economy and Society, 14th-19th Centuries,* (Delhi: Primus, 2019) are the most recent attempts to engage with the Persian Archival records in a significant manner.

Numerous collections of documents from the Sufi institutions like *dargah* of Ajmer, *Khanqah-e Karimia*, Salon, and seminaries like Firangi Mahal and other places having *waqf* institutions/properties and numerous other places at Deccan are available for the critical scrutiny and proper contextualization of the triangular relationship between the State, society/migrant elite, and the ruler overlords. Surely such studies will open up new avenues of research and understanding of the 17th-19th century Persian Archival records in understanding the society and the intellectual tradition in a better way.

III

Literary and Cultural World of Upper Gangetic Valley 'Under Siege' in the Age of Colonial Expansion

The period of 17th century was the most productive as far as the Persian literature is concerned. The empires like Safavids, Mughals, Uzbeks, and the various Sultanates in Deccan and

Central Asia were the chief patrons of Persian literature in their respective domains. The Poet laureates, the official historians, theologians, Sufis, and other literate sections of the society were at their best in producing their best works. By this time the Persian literature has emerged as the most mature form of expressions, emotions, philosophical, theological and liberal ideas. It was the language of the administration; the chancellery has evolved in such a fashion that the most complex branches of knowledge could be expressed in this language with almost a universal acceptability in the Persianate world. Thousands of official documents of various natures including the choicest specimens of *insha'*, *faramin*, *shuqqa* and *parwana* survive in the public libraries, museums and even in the private collections.

'Mughal State' during the 17th century has been described by Late Professor M. Athar Ali as a 'Quasi-modern State' and it has been argued that it has developed principles of governance and even some features of 'a modern State'. The evolution of well-defined Chancellery practices and maintenance of official records emerged as major features of the 17th century governance. The Mughal India had numerous well-defined features for record-keeping; maintenance of the libraries and books at the official level was organized on the scientific lines. These records and libraries were often vandalized by the invading forces; this was irrespective of the nature of the books and records. To recall the diligence and the care with which these libraries were maintained, we need to recapitulate the following instances:

> The royal libraries were maintained by the Mughal emperor and the nobility as well. Zaheer Dehlavi specifically mentions the library maintained by the last Mughal emperor Bahadur Shah Zafar (AD 1837-1857) before the great uprising of 1857.[12] He graphically described the destruction of his own personal library containing a priceless collection,

including twenty very good copies of the holy Quran, transcribed by his grandfather along with seven copies of the holy Quran which were transcribed by his father on the expensive paper made at Yazd and Kashan, and about a thousand volumes related to other disciplines, his collection also included books of history, which his father has specially purchased for him spending three hundred rupees, like *Rauzat us Safa*, *Tarikh- i- Farishta* and *Shah Namah* of Firdausi.[13]

The medieval barbaric acts of vandalism were almost repeated, with even greater ferocity, by the Military Commanders and the civil officials of the East India Company during their joint military campaigns with the forces of Nawab of Awadh during their invasion of the Rohila kingdom of Hafiz Rahmat Khan. The joint action in 1774 resulted into the defeat and death of the urbane and sophisticated Rohilla chief Hafiz Rahmat Khan. He possessed a good collection of books and manuscripts which were captured by the Nawabi forces. 'The whole of the literary treasure of Hafiz Rahmat Khan' was transferred to Nawabi capital of Lucknow. These books were initially kept at the 'Royal library at Purana Daulat Khana and then some of this collection was shifted to the Topkhana library which was closer to the Residency.' This collection included 'some Pushto works written with great care for the brave and learned Rohilla Chief.'[14]

The British campaign against Tipu Sultan in 1799 again resulted in the death of the gallant Mysore warrior and an indiscriminate loot of his capital also included acts of vandalism of his magnificent library which consisted of 'nearly 2000 volumes of Arabic, Persian and Hindy [or Hindustani] manuscripts in all the various branches of Muhammadan literature. Many of these were beautifully written and highly ornamented.'[15]

It was a matter of chance that no less a person than the Alloy Springer, the famous Orientalist, was appointed in 1847 as an extra assistant to the Resident at Lucknow 'for the purpose of cataloguing the extensive collection of the works in Arabic and Persian literature in the king of Awadh's libraries. 'During a period of 18 months 'around 10,000 volumes were catalogued and examined.' An extensive catalogue was published from Calcutta in 1854 prior to the Mutiny. Soon after the annexation of Awadh the deposed king Wajid Ali Shah decided to appeal against this deposition to the higher authorities, leaving the charge of his library, zoo, arsenal and all royal stores in the hands of his trusted servants. However, the English civil and military officials between the annexation and Mutiny were pushy and rude enough to capture all the places belonging to the royalty. It was with a view to erode the authority of the king and his household. They have auctioned the animals of the zoo and have captured all the royal libraries. The hurried manner in which the manuscripts were transferred overnight to the Kothi Martin Saheb was extensively reported in the contemporary weekly newspaper from Lucknow namely *Tilism* and this give us a peep into the damage and destruction caused into the intellectual and learned heritage accumulated during the last hundred years by the Awadh Nawabs.[16]

The Mughal royal household have meticulously maintained their library and have kept the official records in a manner which was quite scientific. We have an idea about the way Zaheer Dehlavi have spoken about his own library and about the library of the royal household. The special officers were designated to look after these collections. Even the noble and members of governing households maintained their private libraries. The fall of Mughal capital on 14 September 1857 came as a calamity for the old establishments. The city lay before the victors and everything was put upside down in an unimaginable manner. The destruction of the loot by the Prize Agents became quite proverbial. The literary heritage of the city belonging to the royalty and private individuals was perhaps worse affected. Many of the collections were destroyed and burned in an indiscriminate manner. However, the following advertisement in the British official channels giveing a peep at the massiveness of the destruction of the accumulated intellectual heritage of the Mughal royalty and nobility in the aftermath of 1857.

> "By order of the Prize Agents, Delhi field force ..... will be sold, by auction at Delhi on the 1st September 1858, 17,000 volumes in vernacular, many of them illuminated. Comprising works on Theology, Medicine and General Literature. The above have been carefully assorted and catalogued and may be viewed.....the day prior to the sale at the house of BHAWANI SUNKER, Chandney Chooke (the present iconic Chandni Chawk).
>
> J H Kerr Innes, Prize Agent.Lieut. W N Lees, Secretary to the Board of Examiners at Calcutta, drew the attention of the Governor General to the advertisement, stating that it ***'adverts to the very great value set upon oriental manuscripts by the European nations, England being the sole exception, and begs that the Governor General may be moved to purchase for the State any manuscript of value which the above collection may contain or the whole"***
>
> ***....4700 MSS were eventually acquired***... good scholars were required to classify and catalogue them...'the cheapest and expeditious means of accomplishing the task was to direct the Arabic Librarian of Calcutta Mohamedan College, with the assistance of two of the senior students, to attend at the College for 3 to 4 hours....for six months.....approval for a reasonable payment covering only *Palki* fare both ways for the Librarian and one way for the students.. Lees should personally ensure that none of the manuscripts were stolen in the course of the cataloguing!

Ironic, it might look, but the facts of such vandalism have been invariably recorded by the English officials themselves. The meticulously prepared catalogues of the manuscripts, astrolabes, instruments and books in the personal collections of the Indian princes and rulers by the military and civil officials of the East India Company bear the sole testimony to the extensive vandalism of the pre-existing intellectual tradition in the various regions of Indian sub- continent.

This point needs to be highlighted for the simple reason that whatever written material, official records and books have survived after British colonial onslaught in Indian sub-continent, it is just partial, fragmentary in nature and even sporadic. A chance discovery of important sources/books and documents keep on coming at the official and private collections. The discovery of *Majalis –i Jahangiri* (compiled by famous Mughal scholar 'Abdus Sattar at Lahore Museum as recently as in AD 2003) has added to our knowledge about the reign of Mughal emperor Jahangir. The students working on the early 17th century were simply unaware even about the name of this seminal work. The other finds like documents, coins and fragmentary material, having a bearing on the society and economy of various epochs of pre-colonial India are almost a routine. The future discoveries of historical material are thus not ruled out.[17]

The present collection includes seminar presentations and conference publications based on unexplored public records in the archives and the private hands. Most of the documents have been accessed from the collection of Acquired Documents at National Archives of India, UP State Archives, Lucknow and Tagore Library, Lucknow University. While the documents belonging to the Salon establishment of *Khanqah-e Karimia* are still in private hands. Therefore, the full deciphered text of these documents has been appended at the end of the respective chapter. The documents referred to in the other chapters can be easily accessed by the scholars working on the subject. However be Fascimiles and transcripts of some of them are also appended after the respective chapters. While this private collection of 'Salon Papers'[18] cannot be accessed that way. Perhaps this justifies the inclusion of Salon Papers as an appendix.

References

1. See Shireen Moosvi, 'Charity, Objectives and Mechanism in Mughal India (16th and 17th Centuries)', *PIHC* (73rd Session), Mumbai, 2012, Pp. 335-346; The modern Indian State have the University Grant commission with its official translation as *Vishwavidyala Anudaan Ayog*, implying thereby that the Universities and higher institutions of learning are being supported by *Anudaan* [*daan* or charity]. Perhaps, it will be most inappropriate to categorize the salaries of university/college teachers out of 'charity'.
2. Donalt Butler, *Topography and Statistics of Southern Districts of Oudh,* Calcutta, 1839, Delhi reprint, 1982, pp. 139-40.
3. Ibid, p. 165.
4. W.H.Sleeman, *A Journey Through the Kingdom of Oudh in 1849-1850,* 2 vols, London, 1858, I, pp.232-4. An abridgement of this celebrated travelogue has been done by P.D.Reeves, *Sleeman in Oudh,* Cambridge, 1971, pp. 128-29, 131-32.
5. The Hanumangarhi episode is mentioned both by Najmul Ghani Khan in *Tarikh-e Awadh* as well as Kamaluddin Haider in *Qaisar-ut Tawarikh,* while some incidents are mentioned in the letters of Mirza Rajab Ali Beg Surur. However, the principal source for our information is *Hadiqat-us Shuhuda* of Mirza Jan, an eye-witness to the episode. Among the modern works an exhaustive study is provided in Muhammad Ayub Qadiri's *Jung-e Azadi 1857: Waqiyat aur Shaksiyat,* Karachi, 1976, pp. 92-116.

see also Jafri, *Awadh from Mughal to Colonial Rule Studies in the Anatomy of a Transformation*, Gyan Publications, 2016, pp. 266-69; Heena, 'Community, Identity and Clashes in Pre-Colonial Awadh: The Movement of Maulavi Syed Amir Ali for Hanumangarhi Mosque (AD 1855)', *Narratives of the Shared Past: Gangetic Valley Through the Millennium, Proceeding of UP History Congress*, Delhi, 2016, pp. 172-181.

6. This section derives much from an earlier piece, titled as 'Religious Plurality in the Chishti Tradition: A Case Study of *Khanqah* at Salon in Awadh', in Jamal Malik and Helmut Reifeld ed. *Religious Pluralism in South Asia and Europe,* OPU, 2005, pp. 219-244; See also my 'The Mughal-Nawabi Legacy under 'Siege' in the Age of Empire [1860s-1880s]: Familial Grants and the Waqf of Khanqah-e Karimia, Salon, India', in Toru Miura ed., *Comparative Study of the Waqf from the East: Dynamism of Norm and Practices in Religious and Familial Donations,* Tokyo, 2018, pp.119-216; The evidence I have used in this paper (my own translations) are reproduced here with minor additions and changes.
7. The evidences from the Colonial records used here have been earlier cited by me in 'Madrasa and Khanaqah or Madrasa in Khanaqah? Education and Sufi establishments in Northern India,' in Jan-Peter Hartung and Helmut Reifeld's (ed.) *Islamic Education, Diversity and National Identity: Dini Madaris* (Jafri 2006, 73-103).
8. See my, ''Indo-Islamic Learning' And the Colonial State 'Bengal Presidency' under East India Company', Historicus Journal of Pakistan Historical Soceity, Vol. LXVIII, No. 2, 2021, pp. 47-68.
9. Shaykh Rizqullah Mushtaqi, *Waq'iat Mushtaqi,* n.d., Add.11633, f.18 and Oriental Collection no.1929, British Museum, British Library.
10. Ghulam Ali Azad Bilgram, *Mathirul Kiram*, ed. by Shaikh Shams ul Haq, *Maktab'Ihyaul ulum e Sharqiya*, Lahore, 1971, pp. 213-14.

11. Irfan Habib, 'Aspects of Agrarian Relations and Economy in a Region of Uttar Pradesh during the 16th Century', IESHR, Delhi, IV, [3] 1967, pp. 205-32.
12. Zaheer Dehlavi, *Dastan-i Ghadar/Taraz- Zaheeri*, Ed. And translated in Urdu by Dr. Afghan Ullah Khan, Sajid Ali Memorial Committee, Gulfishan, Qazipur Khurd, Gorakhpur, 2003, p.42, where he describes *karkhana jat-i Badshahi* [the royal workshops] he very specifically mentions about the royal *kutub khana*.
13. Zaheer Dehlavi, *Dastan-i Ghadar.*
14. A. Sprenger, *A Catalogue of the Arabic, Persian and Hindustany Manuscripts of the Libraries of the King od Oudh,* Calcutta, 1854, pp. iv-v; see also Sir John Strachey, *Hastings and the Rohilla War,* Oxford, 1892, p. 287.
15. A catalogue of these manuscripts was prepared by Charles Stewart which was published from Cambridge in 1809 hastened to add in his preface that **very few of these books were purchased by the Mysore chief. Most of these were part of the 'plunder from Sanoor, Cuddapah, and the Carnatic. Some of them had formerly belonged to the Mohamedan Kings of Bijapore and Golcondah; but the greater number had been the property of the Nabob Nesir Addowleh Abd al Vahib Khan, brother of Mohammed Aly of the Carnatic, and were taken by Hyder in the fort of Chitore, during the year 1780.'** All such volumes were rebound at Srirangapatnam with the official seal, *Sarkar-e Khudadad,* of the kingdom affixed on each volume. A detailed catalogue gives us a hint of each and every manuscript and also provides us a glimpse what books were frequently read by Tipu Sultan himself; see Charles Stewart, *Descriptive Catalogue of the Oriental Library of the Late Tippoo Sultan of Mysore,* Cambridge, 1809, p. v.
16. A. Sprenger, *A Catalogue of the Arabic, Persian and Hindustany Manuscripts of the Libraries of the King of Oudh,* Calcutta, 1854, pp. iii-viii. See also, Heena, 'Communitarian Relations, Colonial Remodeling and the British in Pre-Mutiny Awadh', See

especially the Sub-section B titles; The Royal library store houses and Zoo after the Annexation in S.Z.H. Jafri ed. *Delhi and Awadh during 1857 Studies, Images and Documents*, Delhi, 2019, pp. 191-93.

17. The Persian poetry has been rightly and justly hailed as 'a gift to the humanity and even to the mankind' and it is no wonder that the major works of the Persian poets had been critically edited in standard formats from Iran, they have also been translated in almost all the major languages of the world. It can be asserted that Persian poets and their works are available in all the literary circles. The poetic collections of Hafiz, Sa'adi, Rumi, 'Attar, Jami and 'Umar Khayyam, are universally known. Similarly, almost all the known major historical writings in Persian have been critically edited, both in India and Iran and are available in the standard formats. Major historical writings have also been translated into various languages. The theological and philosophical works in Persian, though numerous but they are yet to be fully available with the same editorial rigors. This can be said for India as well as for Iran, the two major centers extending political patronage to the Persian writers during the 17th century.

    One would like to go back into the previous centuries to understand and also to contextualize the revival of the Persian literature and the social background for the *Persian Renaissance.* It is well known that one of the major fallouts of the *Sh'ubia* movement was the revival and almost a re-discovery of the pre-Islamic Sasanid past. Persian language developed in such a way as to replace the monopoly and domination of the Arabic language as the language of the academic discourse. It must be added that the process was gradual but by the 17th century it was somehow complete. There were few Arabic texts even in the field of theology and religious studies as compared to the texts now written in Persian. The impact of Persian Renaissance was quite noticeable in the Indian subcontinent during the eleventh century itself.

We notice that the first ever Sufi text was written in Persian that too, in the city of Lahore namely Kashful Mehjoob by Sheikh Ali Hujweri {d.1048} it was the growing impact of the Persian Renaissance, it was the growing need of the literally elite of Lahore to have a text on Sufism in a language other than Arabic. No doubt quotations in Arabic, terms in Arabic were freely employed by the great Sheikh. But the principles, theory and the history of Sufism were explained in Persian. Perhaps this experiment also paved the way for the use of local vernacular languages/dialects in the latter writings of the Sufis. The poetry of Baba Hazrat Sheikh Faridud Din Ganj-e Shakar {d.1265} in Multani and Saraiki; and the use of Gurjari in the Ismaili literature and Awadhi in Premakhyan literature are some examples of the way this experiment was carried forward. Though Arabic retained its primacy especially in the theological studies, still Persian and local dialects emerged as important and complementary languages for the dissemination of knowledge, ideas, and ideals in the Indian subcontinent

18. The massive public records of the Khanqah-e-Karimia Salon are not available at one place, they are spread among the various branches of the families which are further spread across India and Pakistan. Moreover, copies of some of these records are buried in the files of the Board of Revenue, UP State Archives, Lucknow. Some of these records have found their way in the files of the Civil litigation for the succession to the office of *Sajjadanashin* and other litigations, especially with *Sunni Central Board of Waqf, UP.* During the course of my research and teaching career, I have made efforts to obtain the photocopies of the Persian records and of the Manuscripts from the various branches of the family. Efforts have also been made to obtain the photocopies from the official files, these acquisitions have greatly facilitated my own researches and has also been used by other scholars in their researches. See also, Claudia Liebeskind, *Piety on its Knees: Three Sufi Traditions in South Asia in Modern Times, Oxford university Press, 1998, pp. 318, 321-22.*

Mughal Officials and the Local Administration

1

A *Farman* of Akbar (1558) from the Period of the Regency

Recently the National Archieves of India have acquired a set of family documents from Begum Amina, wife of Professor Abu Bakar, Jamia Millia Islamia, New Delhi, whose ancestors enjoyed the office of *qāzī* and *khatīb* in *pargana* Chandpur, *sarkār* Sambhal, *sūba* Delhi for a considerable period during Mughal rule.[1] These documents cover a period of three centuries, and mainly relate to property disputes, the division of the *madad-i ma'āsh* holdings among heirs, and initial and confirmatory *farmāns* and *parwānas* for land-grants. There are a few papers from the reign of Akbar which shed light on important aspects of the revenue administration during the period of the *karorī* experiment (beginning, 1574-75). Certain insights are also provided into the problems faced by the grantees (*a 'immadārs*) during this period, which ultimately necessitated the concentration of the *madad-i ma āsh* lands in the certain (*a 'imma*) villages in each *pargana*.

In the present note I only wish to draw attention to the earliest of these documents, a *farmān* of Akbar dated the month of Safar 966, corresponding to 13 November - 11 December 1558.

I first give a translation of this *farmān,* which now bears the number 2719/1 at the National Archives.

[Inovation:) 'He is without need' (*Huwa al-Ghanī*)

[Ṭughrā:] *Farmān* of Jalalu'ddin Muḥammad Akbar Pādshāh Ghāzi.

[Round Seal on the right against the top two half-lines:]

[Legend in middle of seal:] Jalālu'ddin Muḥammad Akbar Pādshāh Ghāzi, son of Muḥammad Humāyūn Pādshāh Ghāzi.

[Names of ancestors up to Amīr Timūr on the rim]

[Text:]

Let the *wajhdārs* [officers holding *wajh*, or territorial assignment in lieu of salary] of *pargana* Chāndpūr know that Maulānā Aḥmad, *Khatīb* (sermon-reader], has come to the Imperial Court and petitined that in respect of the hereditary land (*zamīn-i maurūṣī*), which he holds in the limits of the *qasba* (township) of the said *pargana,* there had been a dispute between the petitioner and Wajihu'd-din, and the said dispute had been placed for adjudication before *qāzīs* of Islam and the reputed scholars of the *khiṭṭa* of Sambhal and (of) the said *pargana*, who gave the petitioner's share to him; but now the said Wajihu'd-din is deviating from that settlement (*dastūr*). Should what has been represented be true, it is incumbent on them (the addressed officials) to act according to the settlement arrived at before *qāzīs* of Islam and the reputed scholars of that place, on which behalf he (the petitioner) holds a public statement (*maḥzar*), and not to allow the said person (Wajihu'd-din) to deviate from that settlement (*dastūr*). Written on the date Safar 966,

The *zimn* (reverse) has two seals, of two scholars Shaikh Anzar, son of Shaikh Khizr, and Shaikh Mir 'Īsā Bābā, son of 'Abdullāh. Unfortunately, the xeroxed copy taken before the document was acquired by the National Archives is not good enough for reproduction. But there are no great problems in deciphering the main text.

The purport of the text is clear enough. The following points however, deserve attention.

1. *Pargana* Chāndpūr was then a part of the *Khiṭṭa* (region) of Sambhal. This accords with the important position assigned to Sambhal by Bābur as a *sarkār*;[2] it later became a *sarkār* of Akbar's *ṣubā* of Delhi.[3]

2. The officials to whom the *farmān* is addressed are termed *wajhdārs*, perhaps a unique instance among the surviving *farmāns* from Akbar's time. This term reminds us of its use in the *Bāburnāma*, in the sense of officials holding *wajh,* or territorial assignments in lieu of salary.[4] The term *wajh* in this sense has a history traceable to the latter half of the fourteenth century.[5] In Akbar's early years the sense of *wajhdār* came to be carried by term *jāgīrdār/jāygīrdār,*[6] and we may, therefore, infer from the occurrence of the former term in this *farmān* that the term *jāgīdār* had still not become universal in 1558, nor was *wajhdār* entirely obsolete as yet.

3. Although the dispute between Maulānā Ahmad and Wajīhu'ddin is stated to be over 'hereditary land', there is little doubt that the land was attached to the office of *khaṭīb*, which too was shared with the other party in the dispute, Wajīhu'ddin. This is shown by an agreement reached on 15 *Rabī*' II 982/4 August 1574 between Saiyid Wajīhu'ddin and Shaikh Ahmad regarding the

division of the duties of the *khatīb* (*qawā 'id-i khitābat*). It was agreed that the *'Īd al-fiṭr* sermon would be delivered by Saiyid Wajīhu'ddīn, and *'īd al azḥā* sermon by the father of Shaikh Ahmad. The Friday sermons were to continue to be shared between the parties in accordance with earlier practice, similarly, 200 *bīghas* of land pertaining to the office (*a'imma-i khitābat*) was now divided equally between the two claimants.[7]

4. The way the dispute between Shaikh Ahmad and Wajīhu'd-din was decided, some time before the present *farmān,* is not without interest. The case was carried for decision not before secular authorities but before an assemblage of the *qāzīs* and scholars of Sambhal and Chandpur. It was, therefore, possibly an informal body that arranged the settlement, which is given here the designation *dastūr*, not generally used for ordinary judgements by the *qāzīs*. In subsequent times such informal procedures came to be replaced by more formal adjudications, so that resort to the former in or before 1558 may be indicative of a lack of administrative control by the central authorities.

5. The *farmān* is written in the semi-cursive *dīwānī* mode of writing usual in Akbar's early *farmāns*, and there is no identifiable writing usual in Akbar's early *farmāns*, and there is no identifiable seal of an official or legible official endorsement on the back (*zimn*). Thus, the case does not seem to have been processed by the *Ṣadr* (minister for revenue grants) as it would have been in later times.

6. This *farmān* was issued during Bairam Khān's regency, when the Regent as *Wakīl* of the Emperor was at the height of his authority. Yet the *farmān* nowhere has his name. This seems to show that Bairam Khān's authority was not formally reflected in actual Imperial orders. Such lack of normal recognition may partly, perhaps, explain why in the later confrontation with young Akbar the Regent's position was so quickly undermined.

References

1. Chandpur and Sambhal are well-known towns respectively in the Districts of Bijnor and Moradabad, Uttar Pradesh.
2. *Bāburnāma*, Turki text, ed. Eiji Mano, Kyoto, 1995, p. 470; Eng. trans. S. Baveridge, II, p. 521.
3. Chāndpūr appears as a *pargana* of the *sarkār* of Sambhal in the *Ā in-i Akbarī*. It was important enough to be the headquarters of a *dastūr* circle within that *sarkār*. See Irfan Habib, *Atlas of the Mughal Empire*, Delhi, 1982, Sheet 8A, 29+78+.
4. *Baburnama*, ed. Mano, p. 553. Beveridge's rendering 'stipendiaries' (trans., II, p. 617) is hardly apt. See also Iqtidar A. Khan, 'The Mughal Assignment System', *Medieval India-I*, ed. Irfan Habib, Mumbai, 1992, pp. 67-8.
5. Cf. Irfan Habib in *Cambridge Economic History of India*, I, Cambridge, 1982, pp. 73-4.
6. Irfan Habib in *The Indian Economic and Social History Review*, IV (3) (1967), p. 209, notices a *farmān* of Akbar of 1563-4, as the earliest document containing the term.
7. See NAI 2919/2.

2

Theologians and Revenue Grantees in *sarkar* Sambhal: Facets of Local Administration under Akbar

Recently National Archives of India has acquired the family documents from Begum Amina wife of Professor Abu Bakar, Jamia Millia Islamia, whose ancestors enjoyed the office of the *qazi* and *khatib* in *pargana* Saharanpur and Chandpur, *sarkar* Sambhal, *suba* Delhi for a considerable period during the Mughal rule. These documents cover a period of three centuries, and are mainly related to property disputes, the division of the *madad-i maash* holdings among the heirs, confirmatory *farmans* and *parwanas*. These includes *mahzars* seeking the removal of the *khatib* from his post, as his not being "aware of the rules and the basics of Islam, will cause distraction in the prayers of the congreagation". There are a few papers from the reign of Akbar which shed light on the important aspects of the revenue administration during the period of the *karori* experiment. Certain insights are also provided into the problems faced by the grantees (*ai'mmadars*) during this period, which ultimately necessitated the concentration of all he *madad-i m'aash* lands in the certain (*ai'mma*) villages of every *pargana*.

The information culled from these documents, is no doubt sporadic in nature and lacks any central theme, yet such cursory evidence can be used to study the problems of the local administration in the early decades of Akbar's reign, without much pretensions I have tried to limit the discussion to the evidence of our documents. Translations of these documents are also appended at the end.

The collection contains an early *farman* of Akbar issued on 7th Safar 966 AH/16th Nov. 1558 AD addressed to the '*Uhdadaran (officials) of pargana Saharanpur, Khitta*' Sambhal. It says that it had been brought to the imperial notice by Maulana Ahmad *khatib,* that his possessions over the hereditary land in *qasba* Saharanpur were contested by one Wajihuddin. The matter was brought earlier before the *qazis* and '*ulema*' of *khitta* Sambhal, who decided the dispute in favour of the petitioner. But Wajihuddin had again started encroaching upon the rights of the petitioner. It was accordingly ordered that whatever had been the decision earlier by the *qazis* and '*ulema*', it should be strictly adhered to. It appears that this time the Mughal state in the process of evolution, the central administration had yet to take roots, therefore, the only way to enforce the justice was to issue the directions to the local officials (who incidentally remain unnamed) to implement the verdict of the local judicial officials. (Document No. 1).

Few details are known about the office of the *khatib* as an independent entity, and in all probability, it was amalgamated later with the office of the *qazi*. However, it appears that during the early decades of emperor Akbar, considerable importance was attached to the office of the *khatib.* Care was taken to ensure the smooth functioning of this office, as among the eccleslastical officers, he was the one having the largest clientele among the 'pious' through his delivering sermons from the pulpit of the mosque. In case of any misunderstanding between the two claimants, a formal settlement was made to avoid the confusion, with the division of the duties, as a necessary corollary, the revenue-free land attached with the office of the *khatib* was also divided to the satisfaction of the claimants.

An agreement was reached on 15th Rabi'II 982 AH/4 Aug, 1574 between Saiyid Wajihuddin and Shaikh Ahmad regarding the division of the duties of the *khatib* (qawaid-i *khitabat*). It was agreed that the '*Id al- fitr*, sermon would be delivered by Saiyid Wajihuddin, and '*Id al-azha* sermon by the father of Shaikh Ahmad. The Friday sermons will continue to be shared between the parties as per earlier practice. Similarly, 200 *bighas* of land pertaining to the office (*ai'mma-i khitabat*) was divided equally between the two claimants, (Document No. 2).

The office of the *khatib* continued to enjoy importance in the subsequent period also. The officials at the *pargana* level took care to ensure the smooth functioning. It appears that apart from the basic qualifications, the incumbent was expected to adhere to certain ethical norms. During the period, we dont hear any thing about *muhtasib* (censure of public morals). In case of any dilution or deviation by the appointee, his replacement was not ruled out. However, such as scrutiny was seldom undertaken by the local revenue officials (*karoris*) on their own, rather he use to act on the basis of the opinion of the learned and of a consensus among them. No doubt, the appointment of the *khatib* and the revenue grant attached to the office, made the institution official, but the fact that his removal involved some sort of the consensus makes it additionally important.

A *mazhar* (statement of the facts) was prepared to the effect that between Wajihuddin and Maulana Ahmad *khatib* dispute has arisen regarding the question of *khitabat of pargana* Chandpur. Wajihuddin was found lacking the qualities and even the capacity to deliver the sermons, therefore, the matter was decided in favour of Maulana Ahmad. After his death, his son Nizamuddin who had the ability and to discharge these duties well, was thought fit for the office. The matter was finally placed before the *karori* of the *pargana*, who also find Wajihuddin and his son, both lacking in the knowledge of the tenants of Islam, and held that their appointment would cause distraction for the pious in their prayers. He, therefore, accepted the suggestion of the '*Ulema*' and asked Maulana Nizamuddin to continue as *khatib* of *pargana* Chandpur, *sarkar* Sambhal (Document No. 3).

It is clear that the grant of land as *madad-i maash* (revenue-grant) to Wajihuddin was only because he happened to be a *khatib,* it seems that though he was removed from post, but the land was not resumed from him. Under what circumstances such a concession was allowed is not clear, but that his descendants continued to inherit the same grant is quite clear. There are a number of *mahzars* and judicial decrees, where the claim of the grandsons of Wajihuddin are put forward or accepted by the authorities, on the strength, of the original grant made by emperor Akbar to Wajihuddin as *khatib*. Does it mean that the descendants were simply using the earlier *farmans* and *tasihanma* to press their claims in an improper manner, or some relaxation was allowed for the dismissed acclesiastical officials to retain the *madad-i maash* grants for their subsistence by Akbar's administration also, there are a number of *parwana* and other papers in this collection from the latter periods where the descendant have claimed the title on the basis of the grant made by Akbar).

Akbar's measure of AD 1578 concentrating all the *aimma* grants in the specified villages is well known. The administrative exercise of such magnitude was undertaken with two aims: to protect the interest of the *makhadims/aimmadars* from the likelihood of any oppression either from the officials of the *khalisa-i sharifa* or of the *jagirdars*; and also present the likelihood only those villages were to be demarcated as *aimma* villages where the grantees had already established *mosques*, wells, house and the *chaupals*. However, we have little specific details as to what actually happened to the grantees before the promulgation of the said order.

Fortunately, three early copies of Akbar's *farman* issued in AD 1775 exist in this collection with fairly detailed statistics. A perusal of these *farman* shed some light on the working of the revenue administration during the *karori* experiment, when large areas were brought under the administration of *khalisa-i sharifa'* and the consequent problems the grantees had to face. The evidence is important enough to be considered at some length.

All the three *farmans* were issued the same day i.e. Ist Rabi II 983/7th September AD 1575, and were addressed to the officials of the *pargana* Chandpur and 'Azampur, *sarkar* Sambhal, *suba* Delhi as these *parganas* were, now included into *khalisa-i sharifa*' and were placed uner the *seh-bandi* arrangement. Such a sudden development must have left the *ai'mmadar* without any means of subsistence. As the order was applicable to all the grantees in general, hence, instead petitioning individually, they represented in batches (*jama'at*) through the *mutawalli* of the *pargana*. The *farmans* were issued to the officials concerned to treat the *madad-i ma'ash* land of the grantees as revenue free with in the frame work of the *khalisa* administration. In all likelihood it was left to the *mutawalli* of the *pargana* to safeguard the interests of the revenue grantees. He enjoyed very limited authority as compared to the one enjoyed by the officials of the *khalisa* and *jagirdars*. This might have necessitated the concentration of all the *aimma* land into the particular villages. That means, the *aimmadars* really required protection from that of the enchroachment of the officials, rather than that they wished to acquire land at more than one place on the strength of the same grant. (Document Nos. 4 and 5).

Detailed statistics are also provided in these *farmans*, which provide certain other clues. For example, we are introduced to different categories of the land, included in these grants. The major category was *maqbuza* (land under the actual possession/use)which included *khud kashta* (self cultivated) *raiyati kashta* (peasant cultivated) and *aqraba' kashta' ibtidai*' (land in the initial occupation) this included *matruha* (land under the thorny bushes) also. There seems to have been no fixecd formula as to what should be the exact ratio of the two categories, while making *madad-i maash* grants.

Similarly, we come across the designation of an officials also, who must have been there for a short while only i.e. during the *karori* experiment, *nazim-i intiqal* (incharge of the transfer of the *pargana* into *khalisa* administration). Subsequently, we dont hear of any such official, in all probability the office must have been abolished when the *karori* experiment itself was given up.

Appendix-A

1. *Farman* of Akbar 7th *Safar*, AH 966/16th Nov. AD 1558

Having *sarnama Hu al-ghani* (he is without needs) and a medium sized round seal with the legend Jalaluddin Muhammad Akbar Padshah-i *ghazi*.

Be it known to the '*uhdadarans* (officials), *pargana* Saharanpur that Maulana Ahmad *khatib* has petitioned to the Imperial threshold that the dispute regarding the hereditary land in the *qasba*' of the *pargana*, with Wajihuddin had been settled in petitioner's favour by the *qazis* and the '*ulema*' of the *khitta*' Sambhal. Now, Wajihuddin is exceeding beyond the *dastur* (settlement). In case this has happened, it is ordered that the settlement affected by the *qazis* and the respectable '*ulema*' of that place as per enclosed memorandum of settlement (*mahzar*), this should be adhered to. It is incumbent upon (Wajihuddin) to know that he should deviate from this settlement and should be guilty of no intereference, written on 7th Safar AH 966.

2. Memorandum of Agreement 15th *Rabi* II AH 982/5th July, AD 1574

The reason for this writing (*nawishta*) is that whereas it is agreed upon and a firm commitment is made to the effect that the duties of *khatib* of *pargana* Chandpur, *sarkar* Sambhal are shared between Saiyid Wajihuddin, son of Bhikan and Shaikh Ahmad, son of Shaikh Mo'inddin since olden times. It is now agreed that '*Id al-fitr* sermon shall be delivered by the petitioner, while '*Id al-azha* sermon shall be delivered by the father of Shaikh Ahmad. The sermons and Friday prayers will continue to be shared by the petitioner and Shaikh Ahmad. Two hundred *bighas* of land are attached as *a'imma-i khitabat* in the *qasba*' and village attached as *a'imma-i khitabat* in the *qasba*' and village Mangar of the same *pargana*. Out of this land, I have taken one hundred *bighas*, the half of the grant: the rest is to be appropriated by the other party. These lines have been committed to writing so that if there be need this could be presented as the proof, written on 15th *Rabi* II 982 AH (5th July 1574).

3. *Ishtihadnamah* Undated, Akbar's early reign

The reason for this writing (*nawishta*') is that whereas a dispute has arisen betwen Wajihuddin, son of Bhikan and Maulana Ahmad *khatib* on the question of the office of *khatib* during the lifetime of late Bangdi Miyan Hatim *Danishmand*, who had decided earlier that Wajihuddin is not capable to deliver the sermons, while Maulana Ahmad had (the competence). Therefore, for some years Maulana Ahmad delivered the sermons (*khutba*') till he died. Now his son

Maulana Nizamuddin, the scholar had acquired the competence (for *khitabat*). The matter was placed a fresh before the theologians and '*ulema*' this time also Bandgi Miyan 'Abdul Haleem and all other *ulema* proposed the name of Nizamuddin for the said job. Finally, the matter was placed before Khwaja Ghulam Husain, the *karori*. He also arrived at the conclusion that Wajihuddin and his son were ignorant of the rules and the tenants of Islam. (hence their appointment) would cause distraction in (congregational) prayers, whoever is in the knowledge of these facts, he may either affix his signature as witness or allow the same to be written down, written in the saced month of Ramazan.....

4. Copy of the *Farman* of Akbar dated Ist *Jamad* II AH 983/ 7th September, AD 1575

Whereas 3088 *bighas* of land, as per earlier *farmans*, is under the possession of Saiyid Shaheen *mutawalli* and his associated (*jama'at*), by way of the *madad-i m'aash* grant in *pargana* Chandpur, *sarkar* Sambal. The said *pargans* is now included in the *khalisa-i sharifa*', therefore, the aforementioned (Saiyid Shaheen) and his associates have petitioned to the Imperial threshold that they possess no other source of livelihood and have large families to support. Since they are found deserving of favour, it is ordered that from the beginning of *kharif* out of total *arazi*, 2634 *bighas* of land and 687 *bighas* peasant-cultivated and self-cultivated from the said *mahal* as per following details, subject to their being in possession and control is confirmed as the *madad-i m'aash* of the above mentioned persons. They should appropriate the revenue year after year and should remain free from the worries of livelihood......It is incumbent upon the present and future '*amils, nazims*, incharge of transfers (to *khalisa*), *karoris* and *istimayan* of the *sarkar* to act according to the *farman*. The *arazi* of the said *mahal* is to be distributed as per following particulars:

12039 bighas
Deduction

pargans Chandpur	*pargana* Azampur
11,989 *bighas*	50 *bighas*
maqbuza (Chandpur)	
11,329, *bighas*	
	Ibtidai' = 615 *bighas*
Chandpur	Azampur
565 *bighas*	50 *bighas*

1230 *bighas* resumed (*bazyaft*) from *pargana* Chandpur

maqbuza	*ibtidai'*
1156 *bighas*	80 *bighas*
	3803 *bighas* deducted

maqbuza (Chandpur) *ibtidai'*

3267 *bighas*	535 *bighas*
Chandpur	Azampur
485 *bighas*	50 *bighas*

6715 *bighas maqbuza* at a separate place

Share of the above mentioned *jama'at* 3088 *bighas* out of which deduct 455 *bighas*

70 *asamis* of these people

Share of Maulana Wajihuddin, son of Bhikan, *Khatib Jami Mosque* and the two '*Ids* and his associates in the environs of the *qasba*' as per details:

160 *bighas*

60 *bighas* deducted

100 *bighas* in *khud kashta* at the old chak

Copied, on 5th *Rajab*, AH 1019/23 September AD 1610

It is incumbent upon the officials not to harass the grantees on account of any dues, and treat the *arazi* free from *mal-o-jihat*, *ikhrajat*, *awarizat* like *peshkash*, *qunalgna*, *sawsri*, *salami*, *jaribana*, *zabitana*, *mehrana*, *muhassilana*, *daroghgana*, *dehnimi*, *saddoi*, *muqaddami*, *qanungoi* and should neither insist upon the cultivation of self cultivated or the land cultivated by their relatives; *begar*, *faujdar*i, *gaoshumari*, *dulaghari* [?] treated as cancelled. This order should be obeyed in every respect and in this regard every years a fresh *farman* or *parwancha* should not be demanded.

5. Copy of the *Farman* of Akbar Ist *Jamad* II AH 983/7th September, AD 1575

Whereas 806 *bighas* of land, as per earlier *farmans*, are held by way of *maqbuza* and *ibtidai*' from *pargana* of Chandpur and Azampur *sarkar* Sambhal as *madad-i ma'ash* of Shaikh Mubarak and Maulana Kamal, *mufti* and his associates (*jama'at*) in perpetuity. The *pargana*, have now been included in the *khalisa-i sharifa*'. The afore-mentioned persons have petitioned to the Imperial threshold that they are deserving favour as they have a large number of the dependents and they posses no other means of subsistence. Since they are found deserving of the favours, it is ordered that from the beginning of *kharif It-il*, the peasant cultivated, self cultivated land and the land cultivated by their dependents and relatives as per details in the *zimn* subject to their being in actual possession and control, the land be confirmed as the *madad-i ma'ash* of the above, named persons and their progeny as per following details. They should appropriate full income to themselves and should busy in praying for the longevity of the Everlasting Empire. The present and the future *'amils, karoris sahibs* [?] of *sarkar* and *pargana* should act accordingly. Be it known that the *arazi* of the *mahal* should be given to the grantees as per following details:

> 12543 *bigha* land granted in *aimma* through the *farmans* which is now placed under the *seh bandi*; out of this the share of the aforesaid *jama'at* of 6 persons is 806 *bighas*, from which 109 *bighas* have been resumed (*bazyat*) in the following manner:
>
> 55 bighas is made over to Maulana Kamaluddin as *madad-i m'aash* for which a *farman* has already been issued (out of this 39 *bigha*' is *khud kashta*', *ra'iyati kashta* etc.)
>
> 54 *bighas* as *a'imma*

Remaining =	697 *bighas*
Maqbuza, Khud kashta and *aqraba kashta*	*Ibtidai* and *Matruha*
387 *bighas*	310 *bighas*
ibtidai - 107 *bighas*	*khudkashta* - 210 *bighas*

pargana Chandpur (*khud kashta, aqraba' kashta*)

647 *bighas*

maqbuza	*ibtidai*'etc.
496 *bighas* out of which 109	260 *bighas*
bighas are resumed as detailed	*matruha* = 210 *bighas*
above = 387 *bighas*	*ibtidai* = 50 *bighas*

Maulana Nizamuddin, the scholar, son of late Ahmad Mo'inuddin and his widow, were granted land in accordance with *farman*' of *Zilhij* AH 965/Sept-Oct AD 1558

3640 *bighas*

80 *bigha* resumed from the environs of the *qasba*

40 *bighas* resumed from the co-shares

40 *bighas* share of the two persons'

Documents from Parganas Sambhal, Baiswara, Cooch Behar and Thana Rangamati

Document No. 1. *Farman* of Akbar AH.9661ADI558 directing the officers of pargana Chandpur for the smooth running of the functions of the *khitabat* as per earlier practice.

۱۴۴۳-۲۷۱۹/۳

هو الغنی

فرمان جلال الدین محمد اکبر بادشاه غازی

بچهره داران پرگنه سهارنپور بدانند که

بادشاه غازی
جلال الدین محمد اکبر

تقوی شعار مولانا احمد خطیب بدرگاه

معلی آمده بدوده عرض رسانید که بجهت زمین و روزی که در سواد قصبه پرگنه مذکوره دارد

خطابت سنبهل

که بیاناته رانج و وجیه الدین مناقشه بوده و قصبه مذکور بحضور قضات اسلام و علمای ذوی الاحترام

و پرگنه مذکوره مرافعه شده حصه رانج را بدو داده بوده اند و حالا وجیه الدین مذکور از دستور

تجاوز میکرده اگر نموده رانج باشد می باید که دستوری که بحضور قضاة اسلام و علمای ذوی الاحترام آنجا

۹۶۴

قرار یافته و محضر درین باب بدست دارد بعمل نموده مشار الیه را بگذارانند که از دستور تجاوز ننمایند تحریرا فی التاریخ شهر

Two seals on the reverse side of the documents with the following legends

[i] شیخ اسلام بن شیخ محمد علوی المتوکل علی الملک ولی

[ii] میر عیسی بابا شیخ بن عبد الله المتوکل علی الملک الراجی علی الله

Document No. 2. The memorandum of Agreement of AH.982/ADI574 between the claimants for the office of *khitabat* for sharing their duties. They also agreed to share the 200 bighas of *madad-ma'ash* land as well.

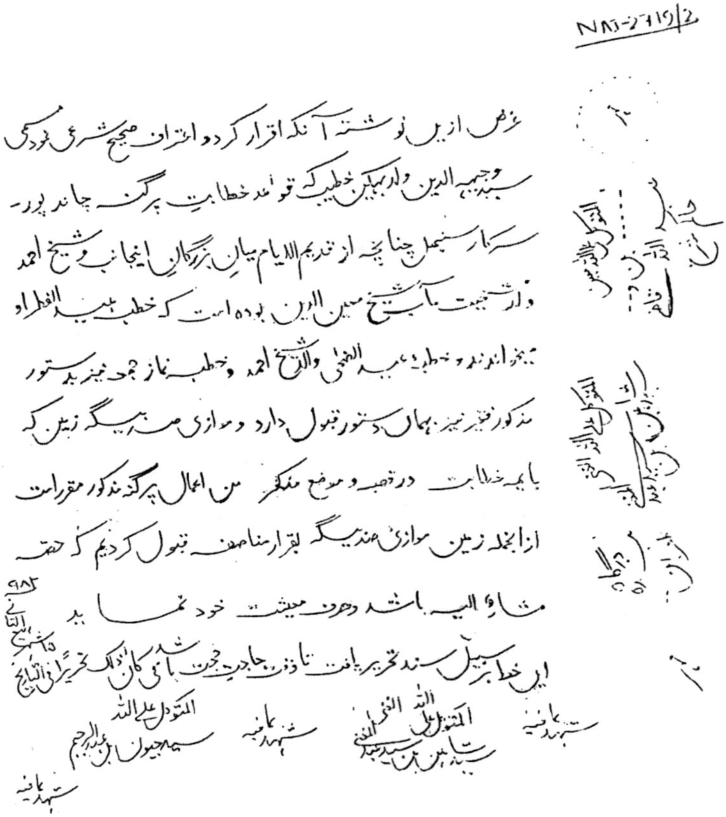

غرض از این نوشتن آنکه اقرار کردو اعتراف صحیح شرعی نمودی مسمی
سید وجیه الدین ولد بهایی خطیب که متولی خطابت پرگنه چاند پور
سرکار سنبهل چنانچه از قدیم الایام میان بزرگان اینجانب و شیخ احمد
ولد شیخ [illegible] شیخ معین الدین بوده است که خطبه عید الفطر او
میخوانند و خطبه عید الضحی و الشیخ احمد و خطبه نماز جمعه نیز بدستور
مذکور فقیر نیز بهمان دستور قبول دارد و موازی صد بیگه زمین که
بابت خطابت در قصبه و موضع مذکور من اعمال پرگنه مذکور مقررست
از انجمله زمین موازی صد بیگه بقرار مناصفه قبول کردیم که حصه
متعلقه الیه باشد و صرف معیشت خود نماید
این خط بر سبیل سند تحریر یافت تا وقت حاجت حجت باشد کان ذلک تحریراً فی التاریخ

Document No. 3. The undated memorandum of details regarding the dispute for the office of *khitabo:* between the claimants as well the settlement arrived at throught the efforts of scholars and the learned people of the locality.

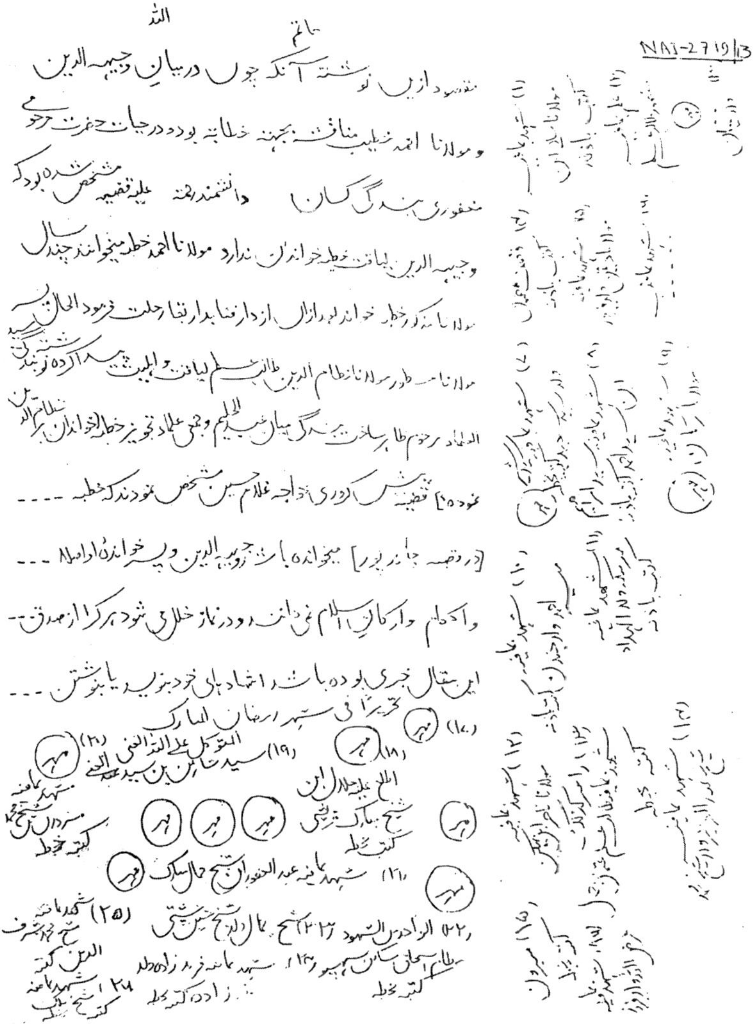
NAI-2719/13

الله

مقصود ازین نوشته آنکه چون در میان وجیه الدین

و مولانا احمد خطیب منافقت بجهت خطابت بود در حیات حضرت مرحومی

مغفوری بندگیان ... دانشمند بجهت علیه قضیه مشخص شده بود که

وجیه الدین لیاقت خطبه خواندن ندارد مولانا احمد خطبه میخواند چند سال

مولانا مذکور خطبه خواند بعد ازان از دار فنا بدار بقا رحلت فرمود الحال پسر

[illegible]

3

Administration of *Jagirs* in Awadh during the 17th Century

If we examine the surviving documents from Awadh during the seventeenth century we would find that those relating to the *jagir* administration are very rare, while papers relating to the *madad-i-ma 'ash* grants and even the *zamindari* rights are quite numerous. This is obviously because the families that have preserved documents have been more concerned for maintaining their claims of the *ma 'afi* and *zamindari* titles, while the *jagir* papers were of no interest from such motives, unless, of course, they are related to *inam* or *atamgha jagir.*[1] Nevertheless explorations at the Regional Records Office (Allahabad), Research Library of the Department of History (AMU) and National Archives of India (New Delhi), resulted in the discovery of a certain number of papers, which, studied together, help to give some picture of the *jagir* administrations as it functioned in Awadh during the seventeenth century.

A *jagirdar* receiving his assignment in an area would invariably be an outsider. The documents show that a *jagirdar* would either appoint his own agents to collect the taxes on his behalf or farm out the taxes of his *jagir* with a view to assuring stable revenue receipts. When the *jagirdar* made their own arrangements by appointing some agents, they used to take the latter's *qubuliyat* (agreement) to collect certain amounts. Such deeds were executed keeping in view the *hasil* (previous revenue collection) figures of the *jagir.* The cost of collection and other obligations of the *jagirdar* were always deducted from the amounts agreed to be paid by these agents. We possess an actual specimen in the form of *qubuliyat* deed executed in F 1116/AD1708 by one Dilawar for a *jagir* in *pargana* Sandila, having a *jama* of 41 lakh *dam.* In all, excluding the cost of maintaining the *sehbandi* troops and *peshkash* to *faujdar,* ₹ 22001/- were to be paid to the *jagirdar* in two instalments.[2]

The *amils* generally belonged to the *jagirdar's* own staff, and were like their masters usually outsiders. One recalls that Charles Elliott on the basis of his own reading of documents relating to the Unnao district, gained the impression that the *amils* "were hardly ever natives of the *pargana,* and did not necessarily hold the office for more than a year."[3] The *amil* had to maintain an armed contingent for quelling any minor resistance to his authority, and in case he met stiffer opposition, he could call the *faujdar* for his help.[4] Very often the big *jagirdars* were also entrusted with the *faujdari* jurisdictions in their respective *jagirs.* The payments to the *amil* was done by allowing him a certain percentage of the revenue-collection, or he received a fixed salary.[5]

The assistance of hereditary local officials such as the *qanungo* and the *chaudhari* was indispensable for the *amil* of the *jagirdars.* They used to present the previous year's assessments, which were accepted in toto, but in case the *amil* asked for a higher assessment, the revision of the previous figures was also done by these officials. Similarly, they helped the *amil* in collecting the outstanding balances from the peasants as per their records, against which there were no appeals.[6]

From some early document (c. A.D. 1619) from *sarkar* Bahraich, it appears that some *jagirdars* used to assign, village of their *tankhwah jagir* to their troopers directly. If in such a village some areas had been already granted to the *madad-i ma'ăsh* holders, the troopers were directed not to interfere with such possessions.[7]

The small *jagirdars,* or those having their postings in a far-off area, always tried to farm out their *jagir.* Certain conditions were imposed upon these revenue contractors or *ijaradar.* There are actual instances where they were asked to treat the *ri'aya* (peasants) gently so that they might remain settled and carry on cultivation. It was thought to be the duty of the *ijaradar* to see that even "one *biswa* of cultivable land should not be left uncultivated."[8] It appears from the claim by a *patwari* (village accountant) that hereditary officials serving in the *ijara* villages were paid their salaries by the revenue farmers.[9] The system of *ijara* had become so popular during this period that even the *a'immadar* or the holders of the *madad-i ma'dsh* grants started this system of the revenue realisation in their villages.[10] The *ijaradar* had no salary or land grant in view of the services performed by him; but, as Butter puts it, "the difference between the sum, which he has for the year engaged to pay into the public treasury" constituted his official income.[11] In case of natural calamities, the *ijaradar* could be provided some relief by being allowed a deduction, and by the *jagirdar* not insisting upon the full amount for which the contract was held.[12]

The terms on which *ijara* of a *jagir* was given are set out in a document of F 1081 : (AD 1673):[13]

> "Agreement *(Qaul-o qarar):* I, Mir Abu Turab, *mansabdar,* affirm that (tract carrying a *jama-i dami* of) 2,100,000 *dam* from *pargana* Hisampur, *sarkar* Bahraich had been assigned in our *jagir* with effect from the beginning of the *kharif, Udi il*, 1081 *'amali.* Therefore, at my own will, I have given the said (territorial) assignment of *dams* in *ijara* (farm) to

Mir Saiyid Muhammad 'Arif in fixed payment of ₹ 2,850 to continue so long as the *jagir* is retained by me, so that he may pay the said amount to me annually according to the following particulars. Should, God forbid, a natural calamity happen, then according to the (official) rate (of remission) for the said *pargana,* I will allow a deduction in the said amount. But, if, by God's grace, more is realised in excess of the said amount, that is left to the said Saiyid."

The following figures follow:

(*Jama*)	
Comprising original	2,10,000 *dam*
enhancement	2,00,000 *dam*
Equivalent, for the year	10,000 *dam*
at 7 months, 7 days	₹ 3,162
Deduct on account of *nankar*	
(salary of officials),	
muqaddam 's pay,	₹ 312
(illegible)	
(Balance)	₹ 2,850

From this document, it is clear that the *ijaradar* pledged himself to pay a certain amount annually to the *jagirdar* – in this case, a fixed proportion of the *jamadami* (7 months,7 days in the month scale of the *mansabdari* system). From this he was allowed a fixed deduction for payment to local officials, etc. This explains the claim of the *patwari* on the *jagirdar.* The *jagirdar* allowed him the profits of the enterprise, as Butter defines them; but the *ijaradar* could claim a reduction of account of officially sanctioned tax-remissions for the locality.

While the *jagirdar* had to make arrangements locally to collect the revenue either directly or through contractors, he had to meet certain obligations to the government. For this purpose the more substantial *jagirdar,* at any rate, used to keep a *wakil* permanently at the imperial court to safeguard his interests and to receive the orders on his behalf. Two very interesting papers concerning a dispute between a *jagirdar* and his *wakil* have survived which shed light on this part of the functioning of the *jagirdar's* establishment. The two documents are translated in Appendix to this study.

One major obligation on the part of the *jagirdar* was the maintenance of a number of animals of standard breed for the imperial stables, providing the cost of feeding them as per schedules and furnishing a number of other supplies under the general name of *khwurak-i dawabb.*[11] It appears that the amount required for the purpose was sent by the *jagirdar* to his *wakil.* The *wakil,* in return paid the required money to the *ijaradars* (farmers) of the *Khwuark-i dawabb,* met the expenses for maintaining the animals (horses as well as elephants) and when the time for maintaining the animals was over, handed them over to the officials of the Imperial stables.

In addition to these duties, the *wakil* was called upon to look after the interests of his master at the court such as getting him a better *jagir.* In the present case the *wakil* was allowed the sum of ₹ 300 by the *jagirdar* to be spent on the business *(muhimsazi)* of getting a new *jagir* assigned in *pargana* Amethi.

The accounts submitted by the *wakil* in connection with these expenses were subjected to rigorous scrutiny. He had to present all the original receipts under the seals of the *ijaradars* of *khwurak-i dawahb* and the *mutasaddis* of *dawabb,* at the time of the audit by the *jagirdar's* officials.

In case of any dispute between the *wakil* and the *jagirdar* regarding the settlement of these accounts, the matter was apparently placed before some Imperial officials. Unfortunately, the exact designation of this officials is not given in our documents; he might well have been the *diwan* or *faujdar.*

The present study does not pretend to give a comprehensive account of *jagir* administration in Awadh. Such an account, given the limitations of our documentary evidence, is perhaps not possible at the present moment. But the above information culled from various documents suggests that enough exists for us to start building a picture of how the *jagir* system as it operated in real life.

APPENDIX

(i) Allahabad-896

I, Buland Khan, *mansabdar* in the *biradari* (clan) of His Highness Diwan Khudadad Khan Jiv affirm as follows:

> Saiyid Muhammad 'Arif held the office of *wakil* at the Imperial Court on behalf of the said Khan. After the termination of his appointment as *wakil* the said Saiyid handed over the *tasihanama* (certificates of contingents) and other documents and papers of *jama-kharch* (income-expenditure) of the *khwurak-i dawabb* to Miyan Muhammad Yusuf, son of the said Khan.
>
> As a dispute ensued, the matter was taken up before Faulad Khan. On this account Saiyid 'Arif presented the receipt *(qabz)* of the farmer *ijaradar* of *khwurak-i dawabb* and *dastaks* (certificates) under the seals of the officials *(mutasaddi)* of the imperial horse stables and elephant stables and other papers, to the agent of Faulad Khan and Ghasi Ram, the (new) *wakil* of Khudadad Khan. However, the case before Faulad Khan not having yet been settled, Diwan Khudadad Khan Jiv and Miyan Muhammad Yusuf maintained their dispute with the said Sayyid.
>
> Now that Miyan Muhammad Yusuf came to the town of Biswa, I took Saiyid 'Arif along to the town of Biswa. Muhammad Yusuf told Saiyid Muhammad' Arif; "Previous to this you had given in writing a *tamassuk* (bond) for

₹ 3000 for the expenses of *badar-navisi* (audit) from the beginning of your term as *wakil* to termination of appointment." Saiyid Muhammad 'Arif replied that *badar-navisi* has not been in accordance with proper norms *(be-hisab)*. Miyan Muhammad Yusuf told Saiyid Muhammad' Arif : *"The jama-kharch* of *Khwurak-i dawabb,* etc., of the period of your *wakilship* have been lost." Now he should submit copies afresh so that the account of his period as *wakil* might be settled.

Saiyed Muhammad 'Arif produced copies of the *jama-kharch* of *Khwurak-i-dawabb* etc. together with receipt *(qubuliyat)* of the farmer of *khwurak-i dawabb,* before Miyan Muhammad Yusuf, Ghasi Ram, Diwan of Khudadad Khan, Shaikh Habib-Ullah the *darogah* of the Court of Justice.

Miyan Muhammad Yusuf allowed deductions *(mujra)* of ₹ 200 which the said Saiyid had paid to Miyan Muhammad Yusuf in *rawal bandi*[15] and also ₹ 565 that Shyam Das, *shiqqdar* of *pargana* Hisampur, had forcibly realised from the village Bedaura of the property and *zamindari* possessions of the said Saiyid in excess *of the jama,* and had recorded under receipts *(wasul)*.

Finally, after disallowing *bazyaft* the expenditure of ₹ 200 on account of Muhammad Khan, *mansabdar* and not writing off the expenditure of ₹ 300 on account of expenses for assignment of *pargana* Amethi, in all ₹ 1,480, annas 5, came out as the balance due to the said Khan, (itemised) as follows :

1. The sum the said Saiyid asked Udai Singh, banker *(sahukar)* of Shahjahanabad, to pay to Muhammad Khan *mansabdar,* and entered as deduction in his accounts of *jama-kharch* not allowed by Muhammad Yusuf, and required to be refunded. ₹ 200

2. The sum Diwan Khudad Khan Jiv had got paid to the said Saiyid for arranging the assignment of *pargana* Amethi, and the said Sayyid truthfully admitted that, without spending the sum, he had drawn the amount from the *jagir* and entered in the *jama* and *kharch* register; he sought condonation, but Miyan Muhammad Yusuf refused to condone it. ₹ 300
3. The balance *(tattima)* in the accounts of the *jama* and *kharch* ₹ 980 annas 5

(ii) Allahabad - 1232

Memorandum:

List of receipts of the *ijaradar* of *Khwurak-i dawabb* and other papers which were given by Saiyid Muhammad Arif to the undersigned Ghasi Ram. 38 sheets received by the signatory, Ghasi Ram (seal).

Receipts *(qubuz-ul wusul)* for ₹ 3128/- 11 annas under the seal and signature of Shaikh Firoz *ijaradar* of *Khwurak-i dawabb* of the imperial establishment *khassa-i sharifa.* ₹ 3128/- 11annas; 28 sheets. *Dastaks* under the seal of official of the *dawabb,* six sheets.

(i) For handing over 10 horses under the seal of Darab Khan, etc., one sheet.

(ii) For handing over one imperial elephant under the seal of Abdur Rahim Khan, one sheet.

(iii) For medicines for imperial elephants, one sheet.

(iv) For medicines for horses, one sheet.

(v) For the straw shed for the stable of horses, one sheet.

(vi) Repairs of the tiled roof for horses, one sheet.

The certificates for monthly payments to Shaikh Firoz, *ijaradar* one sheet.

Qabazul wusul for ₹ 227 received by the signatory, Ghasi Ram, according to accounts, one sheet.

Qabuzul wusul for 8 *asharfis* under the seal of officials of the office for fines on account of absence, one sheet.

Certificate (for receipt) of interest under the seal of the security *(malzamin)* of Miyan Khudadad Khan Jiv, ₹ 1900, one sheet.

References

1. A number of original documents relating to the *in'am al-tamgha* grant of Diler Khan in *pargana* Shahabad have been reproduced extensively by Muzzaffar Husain Khan in *Nama-i Muzzaffari,* Lucknow, 1917.
2. See NAl-1487 (1116F/AD1708).This *qubuliyat* was executed in the presence of village official Jangash Das, *amin, shiqdar* and *mehta,* Kishan Das *waqai 'nigar,* Tilak Chandra, *karkun* and the *mutasaddi* of the Government. The instalments were not equal ₹ 13,200 were to be paid in *kharif* and ₹ 8,890 in *rabi* seasons.
3. C.A. Elliott, *The Chronicles of Oonao,* 1862, pp. 106-7.
4. *Ibid.,* p. 109.
5. *Ibid.,* pp. 106-7.
6. *Ibid.,* pp. 112-13.
7. *Allahabad-789.* The village Kapana was in *tankhwah jagir* of Mirza ' Isa and he had assigned this village to four of his troopers. *A-madad- i-ma 'ash* grant made over to a lady by imperial *farman* was to be exempted from their collections.
8. NAI-1574 (37th RY of Aurangzeb). This *qaul-o-qarar-relates* to village Somb *in-pargana* Sandila, *suba* Awadh in the *jagir* of prince. 'Azimuddin ('Azimushshan) at a total *jama* of Rs. 445/- for the year 1101F/AD1693. The *qubuliyat* was given by Muhammad Qa'im, the *gumashta.* The total *arazi* (area) of the village was 445 *bighas.*
9. NAI-1287 (1254/1838). This *parwana* was issued to the *chakledār* of Sandila to enquire into the complaint of a village *patwari* regarding his pay claims against the *mustajir.*
10. *Firangi Mahal-84* (4th RY of Farrukhsiyar). The village in question belonged to Mulla Nizamuddin and was situated in *sarkar* Bahraich,

while the grantee's residence happened to be at Lucknow. (This collection of *Firangi Mahal* documents is preserved in the Department of History, A.M.U., Aligarh.)

11. Donald Butter, *Topography and Statistics of the Southern District of Awadh and Sultanpur,* p. 99.
12. A *jagir* having a total *jama* of 4,40,000 *dams* belonged to Durvesh Beg *mansabdar* and others. It was situated in *pargana* Hisampur and Saiyid 'Arif held it on a *ijara* tenure. He had agreed to pay Rs. 7,332/- in two equal instalments. See Allahabad-885 *(l080 amali).*

    But the perusal of the receipt issued by the *jagirdars* to Saiyid 'Arif for the same year shows that he paid only Rs. 4000/- (1,60,000 dams). He was also exempted from any further obligation of any subsequent payment for the year.

    See Allahabad-889 (1080 '*amali*).
13. *Allahabad*-884 (l081F/1675).
14. For a discussion of these obligations, see Irfan Habib, *The Agrarian System of Mughal India,* Mumbai, 1963, p. 269 and M. Athar Ali, *The Mughal Nobility under Aurangzeb,* Mumbai, 1966, pp. 50-53.
15. The meaning of this terms could not be traced.

4

Mughal Relations with Portuguese Administration in Goa, 1700-1701: Evidence of Persian Records in Lisbon Archives

The recent acquisition of photocopies of the Persian correspondence preserved at Lisbon Archives, Portugal, by the Centre of Advance Study Department of History AMU,[1] has offered some valuable material on the relations between the Mughal *faujdar* (commandant) of *Talkokan-i-Adhilshahi* (*sarkar* Dhobal*) suba* Bijapur and the Portuguese authorities at Goa at the beginning of the Eighteenth Century. It also offers us an opportunity to examine the position of the *zamindars* or local chiefs who tried to seek refuge with the Portuguese whenever the Mughal pressure became intense. Being conscious of their position to bargain, the Portuguese are seen as trying to extract a number of commercial concessions which, in turn, the Mughals had to concede. A calendar of these documents, prepared by Professor Irfan Habib is appended at the end of the paper for clear understanding of the facts, and each document is assigned a number for easy reference. A map has been also prepared to show the location of all the places described in these documents.

(A) The role of *zamindars* in Mughal Portuguese relations

Most of these documents are concerned with this important aspect. The circumstances as one can see from the documents may be recapitulated as follows:

A group of four *desais/deshmukhs*, descendants of the same grandfather, possessed *zamindar*i rights (*rusum-i-zamindari*) in Panth Antaroj, in *sarkar* Dhobal (previously known as *Talkokan-i-'Adil Khani*) during the tenure of Sarbaz Khan as *Faujdar* of the *sarkar*. When Basalat Khan was appointed the *Faujdar* these *zamindars* (who had been the revenue farmers (*ijaradars*) of the *jagir* of Rafi 'Khan), owned an amount of ₹ 10 to 12 thousand on account of the farm (*ijara*) consequently, one of them Naku Nayak was arrested by the deputy *faujdar* Saiyid Ibrahim. Although he was set free by the agents of Basalat Khan after the death of Saiyid Ibrahim, Naku became a free booter and had killed a number of villagers (*gaonkars*). He alongwith his retainers and members of his caste then fled to Goa. Probably after sometimes, he was joined by Detta Naik also. They began jointly to perpetrate all sorts of "*zamindar*i mischief from their santuary at Goa", by prohibiting the peasants from carrying out cultivation and thus, affecting considerable loss to the Mughal exchequer.

The agent of Basalat Khan, Mushtaq Mirbuzurg informed the Portuguese authorities at Goa of the misconduct of these *zamindars* and requested them to reason with them and try to impress on them the need for entering into settlement with the Mughal authorities. The Portuguese were also informed of the fact although these *zamindars* were realising their perquisites (*wajh-rusum*) fully yet they demanded a fresh *parwana-e-rusum* and the release of the son of Naku (who was apparently kept as hostage, for the payment of the amount which he owned on account of the *ijra*). The power to make the settlement on behalf of the Mughals was delegated to the Portuguese and they were assured that whatever they decide in respect of *rusum*, will be acceptable to the Imperial officials. They should be asked to cease hostilities forthwith, as considerable losses had occured to the exchequer during the *kharif* season and the peasantry had shown its inability to carry on cultivation during the *rabi* as well. If these *zamindars* did not respond to such requests, they were to be expelled from the Portuguese territories at once (Doc. 1). To facilitate such a settlement, the details of the *rusum*, these *zamindars* enjoyed during the tenure of office of Sarbaz Khan, was also provided through Gorakh Sanwi, the *wakil* (agent) of the Mughal official, sent to negotiate with the *zamindars*. The *zamindars* would be paid the *rusum* during Sarbaz Khan's tenure after deducing for harvest losses (*rasad-i-kami*) on their part, the *zamindars* should pay the same *peshkash* (tribute) that they paid under Sarbaz Khan, (Doc. 2).

It seems that for quite some time the Portuguese officials did nothing either to solve the tangle or to expel the erring *zamindars* from their territories, so a high Portuguese official (*hakk-ul-bahr*) was approached by Mirbuzurg. In this letter surprise has been expressed for the negligence and delay in settling such a matter involving the 'Imperial domains'.The root cause of the trouble was Detta Nayak, while Naku is the one with whom negotiations were to be opened as he was the possessor of *deshmukhi* rights (*Khawind-i-deshmukhi*). If they still refused to enter into a settlement with the Imperial authorities, they should be driven out of Goa so that 'the name of the *deshmukh* in the length of Antroj, there retainers and members of their caste, should not remain in Goa'. The cordial relationship betwen the Mughal *faujdar* Basalat Khan and Portuguese officials is invoked again and again. Another official, Ahmad Sarhang was sent to explain the gravity of the situation orally (Doc. 3).

It appears that the strongly worded letter did help, for the Portuguese now acted swiftly and sent a reply soon for which they were promised favours from Emperor Aurangzeb. It was represented to the emperor that "the root cause of the ruin of this country was due to the *rusum* of the *zamindars* and the latter's practice of retiring to the Portuguese territorty." Similarly it was again asserted that no new claims of the *rusum* (over and above those during Sarbaz Khan's tenure) should be entertained on behalf of these *zamindars*. Also no verdict should be given as the actual share of these share holders, but it should be left to be workedout among themselves. The hostilities against the imperial territories had to be ceased in any way. (Doc. No. 4).

The firm resolve of the Portuguese due to the pressure of the Mughal officials, compelled Naku Nayak to agree to the negotiations. He put four demands for the consideration of the authorities, but the official position appears to have remained unchanged–agreement to pay *rusum* as recognised in the times of Sarbaz Khan and an immediate cessation of hostilities.As a special envoy, Ahmad Sarhang was again sent with some additional information to meet the objection raised by Naku Nayak and others. Since the sending of the envoys and emmisaries again and again was a time-consuming process, the Mughal officials thought of appointing the Portuguese official as their plenipotentiary to negotiate on their behalf. The rebels should be told in clear terms that they should not raid the Mughal areas if they wished to remain in Portuguese territory (*mulk-i-firang*) such *muchalkas* (undertakings) had been previously voilated by Naku, but if such things persisted a report would be sent to Basalat Khan, and serious consequences could follow (Doc. 6).

(B) Trade and Shipping

The collection includes a letter addressed to the 'chief Merchants' Viceroy (*Wazrail*) of the post of Goa. It speaks of him in very commendatory terms. It expresses satisfaction that a letter instructing the captain of Diu to hand over the (seized) boat of an unnamed Hindu merchant (*beopari*) of Surat have been received. The Mughals had instructed the *thanadar* of Balasaur (near Daman) not to interfere with the face transit of the Portuguese through the imperial territories, (Doc. 12). In another letter, *Wazrail* of the port of Goa was requested to secure and hand over the ship Muhammadi Salamati belonging to Shaikh Muhammad; a merchant of the imperial port of Surat. Not only this, but they were to ensure that the said ship reached Surat port at the earliest (Doc. 19).

We have seen that the Portuguese appear to have linked their co-operation with the Mughals with their commercial privileges in Surat (Doc. No. 7). In a letter to a Mughal official, *Mir-buzurg* refers to the dispatch of such a *hasbul hukm*, dealing with Portuguese claims to the *mutassadi* of the port of Surat and Saiyyadi Yaqut Khan. This document contained some assurance to Portuguese shipping or commerce since it was expected that the Portuguese would send their vessels to Surat, and the *mutasaddi* of Surat, Yaqut Khan would not raise objections to the *hasbul hukm* on account of "providing escort, lead and gunpowder." Mughal authorities ['] (Doc. 8).

(C) Miscellaneous aspects

A few important aspects of the Mughal administration are also highlighted by these documents. It is well known that the *madad-i-maash* grants were allowed for the maintenance and upkeep of the tombs, mosques and for the running of free-kitchens (*langar-khanas*). Here we find that one Saiyid Qutubuddin was appointed for the *khidmat-i-tauhyat*, or custody of the tombs, mosques, and *langar-khanas* falling within the limits of *pargana* Islamabad (Bhiwandi), and *parganas* Banda and Ponda, simultaneously. Apparently, Saiyid

Qutubuddin's seat was at Kalyan-Bhimri, near Bhiwandi (*Bhimri*).

A *dustak* was issued to the affect that whatever foodgrain was transpsorted from the headqurters to reach Banda and Ponda through Shaikh Muhammad Siddique, the deputy of the *mutawalli* was to be allowed a free passage without any claims for duty, by all officials through their jurisdictions (ta'alluqa) Doc. 13). The document becomes more interesting when we find that Banda and Ponda were located at such a distance away from Kalyan, in different *subas*.

In another document, which is actually a sheet of the *waqia*, we find that Basalat Khan the *faujdar* had applied for the grant of five *mahals* from the *khalisa* (which were at that time under the *ijara* of the *zamindar* of Sondha) to meet-out the salary claims amounting to ₹ 62,000 for his newly raised contingent of 2000 *seh-bandi* troops. It was ordered that the said amount be paid to meet the salary bills of the conditional contingent of Basalat Khan, to be provided by the Imperial collectors (*tehsildars*) (Doc. 15).

There is an interesting letter to Catholic priest, "*Padri Ji Sakrabar* of Goa", in which the writer professes great respect for the *Padri*. Some "known" persons had got two ships manufactured at Goa and was preparing to sail away. Probably in order to prevent him from doing so, the Mughal officials sought the help of the priest to exercise his influence over the Portuguese official (*asad-ul bahar*). There is also a reference to way the letter was sent. At the time the highways were unsafe, and the messengers were not available to carry the post in bamboo-rod (*nalwa*) or cloth bag (*thaila-i khutut*), since the messengers did not want to make their identity known. Hence, the letter was dispactched without a bag. The writer apologised to the *Padri* for this discourtesy.

Notes and References

1. The photocopies of these documents were most kindly provided by Ms. Melba Ferreira da Costs of the Biblioteca da Ajuda, Lisbon. They are numbered Codice 51-V-49, in the Collected Goverreo de Portugal.

2. Such a clause was inserted in an earlier agreement concluded between a Mughal official (Alauddin Muhammad, Hajib chamberlain of the Court) and the Portuguese. It was stipulated that who ever commits treachery (haram khori) against the Mughal Emperor should not be allowed to enter (the Portuguese domains) and should be treated as one having commited treachery against the king of Portugual. The Mughals too have agreed upon corresponding condition. The photographic reproduction of this treaty by H. Heras, 'A treaty between Aurangzeb and the Portuguese', *Indian Historical Records Commissions*, 1927, p. 44.

Appendix

1. (105/189). Letter of Mir Buzurg, agent of Basalat Khan (*faujdar*, Talkokan-i *Adilkham*; see Doc. Nos. 10 & 15 below) to Portuguese authorities (in Goa). The late Sayyid Ibrahim, *Deputy-Faujdar* had arrested Naku (or Nago), *Desai/Desmukh*, from who ₹ 10-12,000 were due to Basalat Khan. Though the writer released Naku, he had now killed many *goonkars* (village-headmen) and prohibited the peasants from cultivating the land. He was practising this "*zamindari* mischief" from his sanctuary in Goa. The Portuguese authorities are requested to reason with him and persuade him to make a settlement with the Mughal authorities; otherwise the Portuguese would tarnish their reputation. Shaikh Ahmad Sarhang was being sent with this letter, and messages to be conveyed orally, No date.

2. (103/179). From Mir Buzurg to the Goa authorities. In order to facilitate settlement with the *zamindars* (who had sought refuge in Goa), Gorakh Sanwi, *wakil* (agent) has been sent with the statements of *rusum* (allowances and perquisities) of *zamindars* in both 'Hindi' and Persian, as these were during the term of office of Sarbaz Khan (two photocopies).

3. (126/207/51. v. 49). From Mir Buzurg to a high Portuguese official '*Hakk al-Bahr*' (Lord of the Sea). Concerns the settlement of claims of Naku Nayak, Datta Nayak, & others, the four *Desais* of Penth Antroj. Points out the good relations between the writer's superior Basalat Khan and the addressee. Yet the writer is surprised that in spite of the request previously made that the addressee should call upon Naku and Dalta to either accept Mughal terms or leave the Portuguese territory he has not done anything in the matter. The root of trouble is Datta Nayak. He should be so driven out with his retainers that, "the name of the *desmukhs* of Antroj should not remain in Goa". Basalat Khan has approved of the writer's proposal that the matter be settled by approaching the addressee. It should be realised that as far as "Imperial Territories" are concerned; none of the retainers of Naku Nayak and Datta Nayak should be allowed to remain in Goa. The addresses should talk to the writer's emissary Shaikh Ahmed Sarhang privately. (No date).

4. (171). Acknowledgment of the above document. Satisfied that the addressee (a Portuguese official) would settle the affairs of Naku Ji. The addressee should feel assured of the favour of His Majesty 'Alamgir (Aurangzeb). It has been already represented to the Emperor that "the ruin of this country is due to the claims (*rusum*) of the *zamindars*, and the latter retiring

to his territory (i.e. Portuguese territory) are causing ruin to the country". The accounts in Hindi and Persian sent with Gorakh Sanwi would clarify in detail what *rusum* Naku and the other *desmukhs* used to receive under Sarbaz Khan. Let the addressee admonish Naku Ji and others not to cause harm to the Imperial Territories. (No date).

5. (102/178/Trad. 177?). Same as above. Acknowledges receipt of two letters, one enclosing a petition from Naku Desmukh and the other through Hira Prabhu, expresses satisfaction. A separate reply is being sent to the four demands made by Naku. Let him accept what was being allowed under Sarbaz Khan. Ahmad Sarhang has always spoken well of the addressee's good intention, and the matter should be settled in consultation with him. The four claimants (Naku & others) should agree among themselves. If they do not mend their ways, the consequences will not be good for them. (No date).

6. (108/209/51-v-49). Same as above. (This letter was apparently earlier than No. 5). The letter sent with Shaikh Ahmad Sarhang, containing details of the affair of Datta Nayak and Naku must already have been received by the addressee. The writer expects that the addressee would call the errant *deshmukhs* and conclude the affair satisfactorily. The four *deshmukhs* of Penth Antroj, viz. Datta & others, are cousins, descendents of the same grandfather. Let the *Deshmukhs* come here with Shaikh Ahmad. However, the matter is settled by the addressee, it would be acceptable. But the *desmukhs* should be told that they must refrain from raiding Mughal territory if they wish to live in Portuguese territory (*mulk-i farangan*). Naku has gone back on the assurance (*muchalka*) he had given. The writer may be compelled to complain to Basalat Khan, so that he be not held responsible for the present situation. (No date).

7. (123/203/51-v-49). Same as previous. Acknowledges receipt of agreement (*ittihad-nama*) from the addressee, (a) stating that in the event of Naku refusing to help in the settlement of the Imperial Territories, he shall be expelled from Portuguese territory, along with his retainers, and not allowed to return, until he settles with Mughal Imperial officials, (b) seeking the goodwill of His Majesty 'Alamgir, and (c) separate dispatch of reply to the Imperial Order regarding (Portuguese commerce with) the Port of Surat. The detailed reply to Naku and Datta has been sent enclosed in the 'big letter' sent to the addressee. The (Portuguese) reply to the Order concerning the Port of Surat was received through Shaikh Ahmad Sarhang on 14 *Sha'ban* 44 R.Y. (24 January 1701).

8. (89/Fl. 163). From Mir Buzurg to unnamed official. Acknowledges receipt of letter from addressee in which the addressee refers to the receipt of (copy of) Imperial order (*hasbul hukm*) to the Governor of the Port of Surat and Sayyidi Yaqut Khan and stating that a ship at the beginning of the season. Basalat Khan is coming himself to suppress "the accursed", Khaman. Is hoped the *hasbu'l hukm* would be complied with, but the reply of the Governor of Surat and Yaqut Khan thereto is awaited. The delay in sending the *hasbu'l hukm* earlier to the addressee, had occurred because, since the sailing season had not arrived there was no need for it. He is asked to get some new boats ready (for the Mughals) and send orders (*dastks*) to the guards of the passes (*ghats*) to let them move between the *thanas* (posts). (No date).

9. (111/188/51-v-49). From Mir Buzurg to unnamed Mughal official. Basalat Khan's reply to addressee's letter sent with Shaikh Ahmad Sarhang. When the Prince comes with the Imperial Army, the dispute over the village Khan Jora would be settled. No date.

10. (132/216/51-v-49). Copy of *Parwana* (order) of (Aurangzeb's principal minister) Asad Khan dated 29 Rajab, 44 R.Y. (9 January 1701). Let His Highness Sadashiv Nayak be assured of Imperial favour. He is required to co-operate with Basalat Khan in fighting Khan Sanwant and the raiders led by Ranu, etc., whom he has sent into *Talkokan-i 'Adil Khani*.

11. (150/151/51-v-49). Najmuddin to Portuguese official. Thanking the addressee for congratulating him on his arrival at Ponda. Refers to good relations 'between the two Kings" No date. (The writer was the brother of Mir Buzurg; see doc. no. 18).

12. (223/51-v-49). (From Mir Buzurg) to "the Chief of Merchants", Viceroy (*wazrail*) of the Port of Goa. Letter addressed to (Basalat) Khan has been received, together with letter instructing "the Captain of Diu" to hand over the boat of *Biupari* of the Port of Surat. The letter has been handed over to the said *Biupari* to enable him to recover his boat at Diu. The *thanadar* of Balsar (near Daman) has been instructed not to interfere with the transit of the Portuguese. Last line cut in photocopy. Dated)–*Jumada* I 43 R.Y. (Oct.-Nov. 1700).

13. (222/51-v-49). Official pass (*dastak*). The custody of tombs, mosques and free kitchens in Islamabad (Bhiwandi), Banda and Ponda is assigned by Imperial grants to Sayyid Qutbuddin, son of Sayyid Shah Muhammad. Whatever grain is sent for the free kitchen from Kalyan Bhimri by the aforesaid, should be allowed to pass by every official through his jurisdiction without claim for duty. Dated 19 *Rabi'*I, 44 R.Y. (26 August 1700).

14. (13/313/51-vii-23). Letter to Catholic priest, "*Padri Ji Sakrabar* of Goa". Has sent news of this place to the Captain of Bassein (Bas'i). Has heard a man has built

two ships at Goa and is preparing to go on them. (No date).

15. (136/217/51-v-49). Sheet of *waqi'a* (official record of Imperial Court), dated 28 *Rajab* 44 R.Y. (9 January 1701). Basalat Khan has applied for assignment of five mahals, which are at present farmed out to the Chief of Sondha, for payment of conditional contingent, with 2000 temporary infantrymen, for the sum of ₹ 62,000. Ordered that the Imperial Collectors are to collect the amount and pay it to meet the claims of conditional contingent attached to office of *faujdar* of Talkokan.

16&17. (137&138/219/51-v-49). *Akhbarat-i Dabar-i Mu'alla*, (Report proceedings at Imperial Court) for 4 & 5 *Rabi'*II, 44 R.Y. (18 & 19 Sept. 1700) (two sheets). No court (*diwan*) held on 4 Rabi'II.

18. Mir Buzurg to unnamed official. Seeks *hasbu'l hukm* (Imperial order) for grant of village Khayora (see doc. no. 9). His brother Najmuddin (see doc. no. 11) is being sent to settle the matter, refers to complaint of a delay in reply from Sayyidi Yaqut Khan. Dated 12 *Ziqa'd* 1112 AH, 45 R.Y. (20 April 1701).

19. (212) Letter to the Principal Merchant, *wazaril* of Goa. A merchant Shaikh Muhammad, son of Shikh "Abdu'r Rahman, has stated that a ship of his, Muhammadi Salamati was sailing from Surat to Bengal, but it had to take refuge in the port of Goa owing to contrary winds and storm. Now, he wishes to bring it back to Surat. Since he is a merchant of an Imperial port, the addressee is asked to make effort to ensure that the ship returns to Surat at the earliest possible in the (sailing) season. Dated 7 *Safar* 44 R.Y. (28 July 1700).

12 lines in Portuguese follow. These may help to identify wazarli, who is also the addressee in doc. no. 12, where his name is spelt Wazrail.

Map. Showing the area *Talkokan-e Adil Shahi* and the places mentioned in the Persian correspondence preserved at Lisbon Archives.

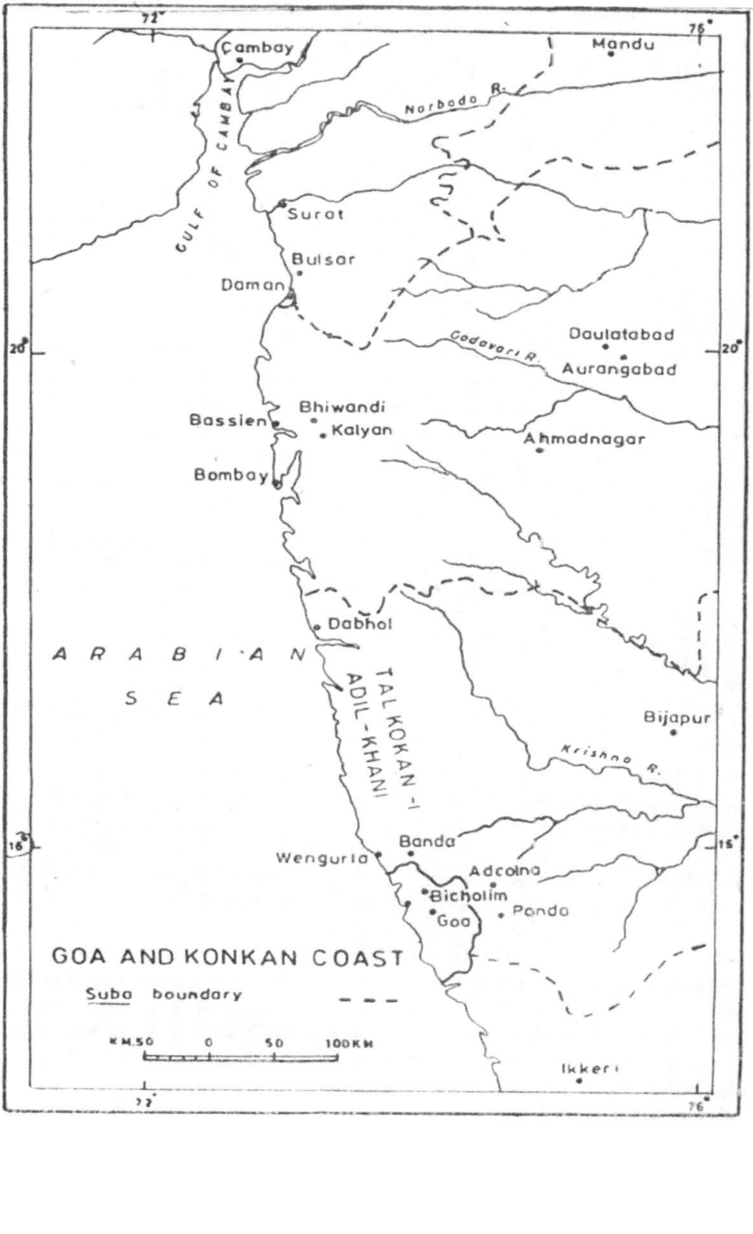

Hereditary Village Officials and State

5

The *Sarkar Qanungo*: 16th-17th Century Documents

The collection of the acquired documents at the National Archives of India New Delhi contain seven documents from the 16th and 17th centuries pertaining to the family of Mathura Das.[1] Most of these papers concern the office of the *qanungo* of *sarkar* Chanderi, *suba* Malwa which ran in Mathura Das and his descendants. The fact that, this family retained the office of the *qanungo* of an entire *sarkar* in hereditary succession for such a long period, beginning from Akbar onwards, makes the study of these documents additionally important. Translations of all these seven documents are appended to this paper.

The first document is a *farman* of Akbar issued in the 41th RY/ 1597 makes it clear. Prince Murad, who was then Governor of Malwa, had sent his own *peshkash* (gift) with Mathura Das, who was thereby able to obtain audience with the Emperor. He was, therefore, confirmed in office as *qanungo* of *sarkar* Chanderi is recorded in the *zimn* of the *farman* as well.[2] This order was later referred to by Prince Daniyal who issued his own *hukm* in accordance with the *farman*, in 46th RY/ 1601.[3]

After the death of Mathura Das, the office passed on to his son Jagjiwan Das. Although the original *farman* of

Jahangir is not apparently presevcd, it is referred to in the *hukm* of Nur Jahan, in 19 RY/1625, by which she too recognises Jagjiwan Das as *qanungo* of the *sarkar*.[4] A new imperial *farman* was granted by Emperor Shah Jahan recognizing him as *qanungo* in the 9th RY/1636.[5] The office passed on to Dharinder Das and Har Rai jointly after the death of their father, Jagjiwan Das. A *hasbul hukm* by Aurangzeb's *wazir*, Asad Khan in 25 R.Y. 1682[6] is of great interest, as we shall presently see. This too confirmed the brothers in their office. Finally, we have a *parwana* issued by 'Adil Khan in 31st RY/1688, granted in favour of these two brothers. Three generations of these *qanungos* thus, practically spanned the century.[7]

These documents are of great value as making us familiar with *qanungos* of *sarkar*, as against of *parganas*, who have generally received notice from historians.

The conferment of the office of the *qanungo* of an entire *sarkar* does not mean that there were no *qanungos* left at the *pargana* level. As Asad Khan's order specifically refers 'to the *qanungos*' of the *parganas* of *sarkar* Chanderi; among the addresses, while conveying Imperial orders in favour of Dharinder Das and Har Rai as *qanungos* of the *sarkar*.

A persual of these documents spell out the details of the duties which these *qanungos* were expected to perform. These related to the sending of details of the conditions of the *ri'aya*, the *muzari'an* and other residents of the *sarkar* to the Court. After necessary elucidation and collation the *qanungo* was expected to forward the current year's *taqsim* (paper relating to area) *hal-o hasil* (revenue-realization) and *mawazina* (revenue-collection of previous years, usually ten) papers to the office of the central diwn (*daftar-i Khana-i' Ala*).[8]

Similarly, it was incumbent upon them not to realize illegal taxes like *ikhrajat* and *malba* from the peasantry.[9] Another interesting fact which emerges from the *farmans* of Akbar and Shahjahan that the *qanungo* of the *sarkar* was to keep one of his brothers or kinsmen at the Imperial Court to enable the headquarters to obtain information immediately.

Chanderi was a very large *sarkar*. According to the Ain it had no less than 61 *mahals* (or *parganas*). It contained, besides Chanderi, the well-known town of Sironj.[10] Here Jagjiwan Das settled a village named after himself (Jagjiwanpur) which was later assigned to him in *in'am* (tax-free) by 'Iwaz Muhammad Khan, probably a *jagirdar* of the *pargana*, in AH 1034 / AD 1625.[11] Similarly, the *hukm* of Nur Jahan of 19th RY/1625 refers to the establishment of *katra* (market) in Sironj town, prudently named Nur Gunj, by Mathura Das. The income from this *katra* was assigned to Mathura Das's son, Jagjiwan Das by Nur Jahan, and the *jagirdars* and others were directed not to interfere with the merchants (*beoparis*) coming to this market.[12]

The most interesting of these documents is the *hasb-ul hukm* issued by Asad Khan in AD 1682. This document tells us that a general order has been issued for the dismissal of all *qanungos* of *sarkar* by Aurangzeb. The reason for this is not stated in the text, but the *zimn* tells us that this order followed the discovery of certain facts about the office of the *qanungo* of *suba*. Thatta, when it was held by Muhammad Sharif titled Qabil Khan. Now, Muhammad Sharif Qabil Khan was the *mir-munshi* of Aurangzeb when he was the viceroy at Deccan and he was the draftsman of the letters of Aurangzeb collected in the volume called *Adab-i Alamgiri*. His dismissal from the office of the *qanungo* of *suba* Thatta is noticed in Saqi Musta'id Khan's *Maasir-i'Alamgiri* under the 23rd RY/1680-1 of Aurangzeb.

We are informed that,

"Qabil Khan, *mir-munshi,* the brother of Abul Fath, Qabil Khan of Thatta, an old imperial servant, who because of his past service and proximity to the imperial person had been awarded promotions and favours. Because of evil fate he deviated from the right path. He was dismissed from the *mansab* of 1000 zat/70 *sawar* and the office of *taqqarrub-i zaria*' and *qanungoi* of the *suba* Thatta, along with his son-in-law Abdul Was's on his own application, he recived the permission to go to Court.[13]

Apparently, Aurangzeb decided that *qanungos* above the *pargana* level were not of much use; and Qabil Khan's unknown misdemeanour were probably ascribed to the mischief that *qanungo* at the *sarkar* level could create. It was probably, felt that all the necessary information could be obtained from the *qanungo* of *pargana* directly by the diwan.

Nizamuddin Ahmad, *diwan* of *suba* Malwa, however, recommended that in the cause of *sarkar* Chanderi the order of dismissal may not be implemented. He refers to the fact that the *sarkar* of Chanderi was assigned in *jagir* to the local Rajput *zamindars* who evidently tended to treat the area as their *watan*. It will be seen from the *Ain-i akbari* that a large number of the *mahals* in *sarkar* Chanderi had the *jama*' in round figures. Out of 44 named *mahals*, only 14 *mahals* have exact numbers (i.e. they do not have zeros as their last three digit). This forcefully suggests the presence of the Chiefs. Among these eighteen parganas have Rajput *zamindars*. The *diwan* urged that if the office of the *qanungo* of the *sarkar* was abolished, it would be very difficult to collect the necessary information about the assessment and collection (*jama' wa wusul*), within the *sarkar*. The *diwan's* argument prevailed and the Emperor approved the continuation of the office of *qanungo* in the *sarkar*, which was then shared by the two sons of Jagjiwan Das.

It is worth noting that but for our document, the important measure ordered by Aurangzeb of the removal of the *qanungos* of *sarkar* throughout the empire would not have been known to us.

Appendices

(Following are the translations of the documents)

Appendix-I NAI 2371 (*Farman* of Akbar, A.D. 1597)

Invocation : God is Great

Seal : Jalaluddin was Duniya Akbar Padshah

Tughra : *Farman* of Jalaluddin Muhammad Akbar *Padshah Ghazi*

Whereas Mathura Das, *qanungo* of *sarkar* Chanderi was permitted to kiss the Imperial threshold through the good offices of Princes (Murad) (titles omitted) and has represented that the office of the *qanungoi* of the said *sarkar* has belonged to him from his ancestors since olden times; therefore, he has been favoured by the issue of this *farman* to the effect that the office of the *qanungo* of the said *sarkar* be enjoyed by him as heretofore and that he should perform the duties of the office with all due care. He is to report correctly every season the conditions of the *ri'aya* (peasants), *muzari'an* (cultivators) and the residents (*sakna wa mutawattinan*) of the *sarkar* to the exalted court. He should depute one of his brothers or kinsmen to the court so that he may, remaining at the court, inform it (of the said conditions). It is requisite on the part of the *jagirdars*, *karoris zamindar chaudaris* (so written) *muqqaddams*, peasants and cultivators of the *parganas* of *sarkar* Chanderi to recognise him as the *qanungo* of that sarkar and accede to his authority in matters pertaining to the said office; and should not let important matters be settled without his knowledge and advice. Whatever is spoken by him regarding the collection of land-revenue (*mal-o jihat*) and the amelioration of their conditions should be accepted as trustworthy; and they should not let anyone else claim to be his co-sharer (in the office) and the revenue should be delivered to him. This order should be strictly adhered to, and nothing contrary be done. Dated *Uzram* 21 *Isfandaz Ilahi* 41th R.Y.

Zimn

Details of *talliqa*

Ordered on *Imardad*, 7th *Aban Ilahi* 41st RY/Tuesday 1005 AH. Mathura Das, who had brought the *peshkash* of Prince (Murad) (title omitted). Let the office of *qanungo* of *sarkar* Chanderi be retained by him as heretofore. Written by Khwaja Mathura Das *musharif* of the *mahal*, during the guard-duty (*chauki*) of Baba Aibak, and the turn of the *waqia nawis*, Maulana Nazr.

Endorsement: This is according to the *waqia* written by me, Nazr.

Written by Khwaja Mathura Das, *musharraf mahal*, at the Chauki of Baba Aibak.

Seals: (i) *Khan-i Khanan*, Murad of Akbar Shah AH 993.

(ii) His slave, Kamaluddin Husain

(iii) Asaf Khan AH 1005.

Appendix-2 NAI 2372 *Hukm* of Daniyal, AD 1601

Invocation: God is Great

Seal: Daniyal Akbar Shah 1005

Tughra : *Hukm* of Sultan Daniyal (son of) Shah Akbar

Whereas according to the exalted *farman*, the office of *qanungo* of Sarkar Chanderi has been bestowed upon Mathura

Das and he has represented that he has worked hard in the matters of the welfare of the *ria'ya* of the mahal (of *sarkar* Chandri) and for raising of the income of the Government and managing other affairs, therefore, it is ordered that the said office would continue to be held by him so that holding firmly that office, he should take full care and correctly report every season the conditions of the *ria'ya*, *muzarian*, *zamindars* and all other residents of the area to the exalted court and try hard for increasing the population and prosperity of that *sarkar* and not allow *malbu*' and *akhrajat* (taxes) to be extracted from the *ri'aya*. It is requisite that the *jagirdars*, *karoris*, revenue-collector ('*ummals*), *mutasaddis*, *zamindars*, *chaudharis ri'aya*, *muzarian* and all the residents of the *parganas* of the said *sarkar* should recognise him as the *qanungo* of that *sarkar*, and accede to authority fully in the said matters and should not perform important business without his knowledge and advice and whatever he speaks regarding the raising of the revenue, amelioration of the conditions of the *ri'aya* and the extension of the cultivation and habitation in the said *sarkar* should be regarded as trustworthy, and all the perquisites associated with this office should be paid to him, without any co-sharer or partner, and should not permit any one to interfere with him in the said matters. This order is to be followed strictly without any deviation. Dated 15th *Ardishahar Ilahi* 46th/A.H 1009.

Appendix-3 NAI 2373 *Hukm* of Nur Jahan, AD 1625.

Innovation: God is Great

Seal: Nur Jahan *Begum-i Padshah-i Dauran*

Tughra: *Hukm* of Nur Jahan *Begum-i Padshah*

Whereas according to the exalted *farman* of Jahangir, the office of the *qanungo* of *sarkar* Chanderi, *suba* Malwa has been assigned to Jagjiwan Das, son of Mathura Das; It is incumbent upon the *hukkam 'ummal*. and the *mutassadis* of the present and the future, of the said *sarkar* to recognise him as *qanungo*, and accede to his authority fully in the said matters, (and should not perform important business without his knowledge and advice) and whatever he speaks regarding the raising of the revenue, amelioration of the conditions of the *ri'aya* (None of the addresses) should deviate from it in the least. It was also ordered that since Mathura Das, father of the aforesaid person had constructed *katra* Nurganj in *qasba* Sironj, the task of making the said *katra* populous has been entrusted to Jagjiwan Das. It is incumbent upon the *jagirdars* and the residents of the said *qasba* to allow the traders (*beoparis*) to bring and deal in *kothari* goods in the said *katra* and other transaction (they) should not be harrassed by any one. These orders are to be adhered strictly without any deviation of these command. Dated 17th *Bahman Ilahi* 19th R.Y.

Appendix-4/NAI 2374/*Parwana* of Iwaz Muhammad, AD 1625 AD

Innovcation: God is Great

When this servant of His Majesty arrived at Sironj, I became aware of the efficiency and loyalty of Jagjiwan Das. Therefore, the village Jagjiwanpur was granted to him by way of *in'am* from the beginning of *kharif ud* II 1033 on condition that he would strive daily for the increase of revenue, increase in population and prosperity of the said *pargana*. God willing, he shall be rewarded according to service rendered by him. Dated 26 *Jumada* I 1034 A.H.

Appendix-5 NAI 2375/*farman* of Shah Jahan, AD 1736

Invocation: God is Great

Tughra: *Farman* of Abul Mazaffar Shahabuddin Muhammad Shah Jahan, *sahib- qiran-i sani*, *padshah-i ghazi*.

Seal: A big lineal square seal of the Emperor in middle, and circle with the names of his ancestors in small circles around, beginning from Timur.

Whereas *Umdatul Mulk* (*Khan-i Dauran*) presented Jagjiwan Das son of Mathura Das (before the Emperor) and he has represented to the sublime court that according to the exalted *farman* of Emperor *Jannat Makani* (Jahangir) the office of the *qanungo* of *sarkar* Chanderi vests with him and he has solicited that an imperial *farman* be granted to this effect, the word subduing order has, therefore, been issued that the office of the *qanungo* of *sarkar* Chanderi *suba* Malwa should vest with him, as heretofore, in accordance with the zimn so that he should strive his utmost for the execution of the duties pertaining to the said post, make sincere efforts for the extension of cultivation of that area, send to the office every year the *taqsim* (area) and *hal-i hasil* (revenue realisation) papers of the parganas of the said *sarkar*, set in detail and accurately. It is incumbent upon the *hukkam* (officials), '*ummal* (revenue-collectors), *jagirdars*, and *karoris*, present and future, *chaudharis*, *zamindars*, *muqqadams* and *muzari'an* (cultivators) of the said *sarkar* to abide by the imperial order, recognize him as the *qanungo* of the area in the same way as his father, accede to his authority in all matters relating to that office, and rely on whatever he says for the larger income of government and the well being of the peasantry. They should not permit anyone else to share the office with him, if he is not an heir (of Mathura Das) and does not have a *sanad*, nor should they undertake matters within the jurisdiction of that office without his knowledge. It has also been ordered one of the brothers or relative of Jagjiwan Das should be present all the time at the imperial headquarters (*rakab-i huzur*) as to keep the court informed about the affairs of that *sarkar*. No fresh *farman* or *parwana* should be demanded every year in this regard and there should be no deviation from what has been ordered. Dated *Urdibihisht Mah Ilahi* 9/15 *Ziqa'ad* 1045 Hijri.

Zimn

Y*addashjt-i waqi'a* dated 14th *Isfandyar*, 9th *Ilahi*/ Thursday, 14th *Rmzan* AH 1045 recorded upon the report (*risala*) of Afzal Khan (titles omitted) and at the turn of Ali Naqi (the recorded of the *zimn*) as waqi'a navis. Whereas the office of *qanungoi* of *sarkar* Chanderi vests with Jagjiwan Das, son of Mathura Das, according to a *farman* of His Majesty (Emperor Jahangir) and now His excellency *Khan-i Dauran* has presented him before Emperor and it has been represented to the Emperor that he solicits the issue of a new *farman*. Therefore, the word-subduing order has been issued that ......(henceforward practically the same text as in the main *farman*, and so omitted here). Within accordance with the Confirmed Copy of Record (*Tasdiq-i yaddasht*).

Endorsement in the writing of His excellency Afzal Khan (titles omitted): "Let it be recorded in the *waqi'a* Endorsement in the writing of the *waqia'nawis*: "Text is in accordance with the *waqi'a*."

Endorsement in the writing of His Excellency with the *waqi'a* (Afzal Khan); Let it be put up for confirmation (*'arz-i mukarrar*).

Endorsement in the writing of *'Abdu-r Rahman*: "On 26 *'Asfandarmuz*[8] (*Ilahi*) was put up for confirmation (before His Majesty")

Endorsement in the writing of His Excellency (Afzal Khan) (titles omitted): "Let the *farman* be Prepared".

Seals—(i) Mir Jumla, *Banda-i Shah jahan*

(ii) Afzal Khan *Dil-o Jan-i Shahjahan*

(iii) Bande Das Ghulam Shahjahan Padshah

(iv) Kadev Sen *Banda-i Shahjahan*

(v) A small but undecipherable seal.

Appendix-6 NAI 2376 *Hasbul Hukm* of Asad Khan, AD 1682.

Invocation: He is Rich!

Seal: Asad Khan, Murid Shah' Alamgir

Be it known to the officials, administrators, governors, revenue-collectors, *jagirdaras*, and *karoris*, present and future, *chaudhuris*, *qanungos*, *zamindars*, *muqqadams*, peasents and cultivators of the *parganas* of *sarkar* Chanderi, *suba* Malwa, that the office of the *qanungo* of the said *sarkar* had been held by Jagjiwan Das, son of Mathura Das, in accordance with the *farmans* of Emperors ... . (Akbar) ..... (Jahangir) and ......(Shah Jahan), and he is now deceased. His sons, Harinder Das and Har Rai, performed the duties of his post after his death. Subsequently, the imperial orders were promulgated that the *qanungos* of *sarkars* be dismissed throughout the Imperial dominions, and so they too were removed.

Whereas now Nizamuddin Ahmad *diwan*, *suba* Malwa has certified to the Imperial Office, as under his seal to their efficiency and loyalty and written that they have always been obedient to the Governor of the *suba* and the *Diwan*, and sent the registers to the Imperial Office, and since most of the *parganas* of the said *sarkar* are in the *jagirs* of the Rajput *zamindars*, no information can be gathered regarding the details of the *jama*' (assessment), *wusul* (realization) and other circumstances of these *parganas* of the *sarkar* of Chanderi, without there being a *qanungo* of the *sarkar*, it would be useful if the office of *qanungo* of *sarkar* Chanderi is allowed to vest with Dharindar and the Har Rai as of old. Therefore, the imperial order has been issued that the office (of *qanungo* of) *sarkar* Chanderi be vested with Dharinchar and Har Rai as of old. It is requisite that they (the addressees) should recognise them to be *qanungos* of the said *sarkar* and consider them to possess full authority in matters of that office, and should not deviate from the advice and counsel of the said persons, when it is in every way conducive to the financial advantage of the government, and the well-being and welfare of the peasantry and the maintenance of habitation. the said persons (i.e. the *qanungos*) should so conduct themselves that the official register of *taqsim* and *muwazina* and other papers are sent to the Imperial Office in accordance with the requirements of the *Diwan*, and the peasants and all people are kept happy by their own good behaviour. Date I *Muharram*, 25 Regnal Year.

Zimn

Office of *qanungo* of *sarkar* Chanderi, *suba* Malwa, conferred on Dharindar Das and Har Rai according to the letter of Nizamuddin Ahmad, *diwan* of the *suba* approved by the Emperor.Text Representation of Nizamuddin Ahmad, *diwan* of *suba* of Malwa being letter under his seal handed over to office, to the effect that the office of the *qanungo* of *sarkar* Chanderi, *suba* Malwa has been occupied under *farmans* of Emperors Akbar, Jahangir and Shah Jahan. When the facts concerning the office of *qanungo* of *suba* Thatta, held by Muhammad Sharif titled Qabil Khan, reached the Imperial Court, the *qanungos* of *sarkars* in certain *suba*s were ordered to be dismissed. (But) since these (*qanungos* of *sarkar* Chanderi) have always been obedient to the Governor of the *suba* and the *diwan* and submitted registers to the office (regularly) and most of the *parganas* of *sarkar* Chanderi are in the *jagirs* of Rajput *zamindars* the papers for these *mahals* (*parganas*) cannot reach the office in an accurate form without their being a *qanungo* of the *sarkar*. If the said office remains vested in Dharindar and Har Rai, son of Jagjiwan Das, as of old, this would be helpful. They are in possession of *razinama* (expression of consent) from the *jagirdars* and the *ri'aya*.

Seal–One small seal of Asad Khan *Murid Shah 'Alamgir*, at the right hand margin of the front of *parwana*.

Endorsement at the back—

(i) Entered in the *siyaha*, dated 9th *Muharram* 25th R.Y.

(ii) Copied at the *sarrishta* of the *suba*

(iii) Copied at the office of *taqsim-i mumalik-i mahrusa*, dated 11th *Muharram* 25th R.Y.

(iv) According to the *siyaha* of the officials.

(v) Seen.

Appendix-7/NAI 2377/Parwana of 'Adil Khan, AD 1688.

The revenue-collectors (*'amils*), *chaudhuris*, *qanungos*, cultivators (*muzari'an*) etc. of *pargana* Raga, *sarkar* Chanderi, *suba* of Malwa, are to know that according to the orders (*hasb-ul hukm*) of His Excellency Asad Khan and the *sanads* of the governors (*hukkam*), the office of *qanungo* of the said *sarkar* has been vested in Dharindar Das and Har Rai. Therefore, it is written that whatever customary dues of the office of *qanungo* the said persons have been collecting, they should be allowed to collect according to custom so that they may send the register of papers (regularly to) the Court, under their own signatures, after preparing them correctly. They should follow this rigorously, Dated I *Rabi*'II, 31st Regnal Year.

Seal—One small seal of 'Adil Khan, *banda-i Shah Alamgir*, at the right hand margin of the front of *Parwana*.

Notes and References

1. Accession Numbers 2371 to 2377 (Oriental Records Division), hereafter referred to by numbers following letters NAI. I am most grateful to Mr. Zakir Husain, Archivist (OR Division) National Archives of India for helping me in deciphereing a number of seals, endorsements, and details of the *zimn*.
2. NAI 2371.

3. NAI 2372. This has been published with translation by S.A.I. Tirmizi, *Edicts From the Mughal Haram*, IA Delhi, 1979, pp. 28-29 for photoplate and deciphered text; pp. 30-32 for translation and notes.
4. NAI 2373.
5. NAI 2375.
6. NAI 2376.
7. NAI 2377.
8. For an explanation of these terms see Irfan Habib, *Agrarian System of Mughal India*, Mumbai, 1963, especially pp. 178 & n. 203-4, 206 & pp. 263-64.
9. Every tax, or levy paid by the village in addition to the land revenue, was concerned under these taxes. These included the share claimed by the village officials, *zamindars* and expenses incurred in the 'Common pool' of the village. See for details, Irfan Habib, *Agrarian System*, pp. 126-7, 243 & n.
10. Abul Fazl, *Ain i Akbari*, Bib. Indica I, pp. 457-61; although the total number of the *mahals* are stated to be 61, but the names of only 44 *mahals* have been furnished. Of these 31 have been located in Irfan Habib; *An Atlas of the Mughal Empire*, P, 1982, Sheet No. 3A, 6A and notes.
11. NAI 2374.
12. NAI 2373.
13. Saqi Mustra'idd Khan, *Ma'astr-i 'Alamgiri* Bib, Indi. ed. Kolkata 1870-73, pp. 190-1.

6

Side Lights on Administrative Structure and Agrarian Relations in Awadh: A Study of Laharpur Documents (16th-18th Century)

A *Qanungo* Family of Laharpuri

The Tagore Library of Lucknow University (abbreviated on LUL flowed by accession number) contains a number of 16th-18th centuries Persian documents belonging to *pargana* Laharpur *sarkar* Khairabad *suba* Awadh.[1] The area is now located within the limits of modern district Sitapur.[2] These papers include *farmāns*, *parwanās*, statements in case of disputes and petitions. Most of these papers relate to the family of a Shaikh, which settled here during the time of Mughal empror Akbar in this area and enjoyed the *qanungai* rights over 5 *tappa*. With the passage of time the family acquired some land by way of *madad-a-maash* and *zamindāri* rights as well.

The office of the Qanungo: Most of the papers of this collection relate to the office of the *qanungo* in five *tappa* of *pargana* Laharpūr, namely *haveli* Laharpur, Mankapur, Devpalpur and Kharij.[3] A number of citations in the official *parwanas* and other documents make it abundantly clear that Akbar recognised the existing rights of the office of *qanungo* of one Shaikh Mazhar.[4] Although the original title deed is missing from the collection, but his dispute with *naib-muqqadam* on the question of some agrarian perquisites of certain villages, finds mention in an early *farmān* of Akbar issued to Umdatul Mulk Nizamuddin Muhammad Dost Khan in AD 1571.[5] In the course of time the office seems to have become hereditary as it passed from father to son and from brother to brother. The geneological tree of the family can be worked out on the basis of the various documents in the collection.[6]

1. Shaikh Mazhar
2. Shaikh Muhiuddin, son of 1
3. Shaikh Hamid, son of 2
4. Shaikh Naim son of 3
5. Shaikh Muhammad Inayat, son of 4
6. Shaikh Rahmat Ullah son of 5
7. Shaikh Haibat Ullah, brother of 6
8. Shaikh Ghulam Rasool, brother of 7
9. Shaikh Muhammad Ashiq son of 6

It appears that on occasions, the fortunes of the family were threatened by the local potentates, hence, *parwana* were issued a fresh recognising the exclusive rights of the members of the family and protecting their rights from being encroached upon. An interesting *parwana* issued by Khair Andesh Khan in 25th *Ry* of Aurangzeb recalls a representations by the *wakil* of Shakh Rahmat Ullah to the effect that the 'Hindu *Chaudharis* and *qanungo* of the area always put their signatures over the *tumār-i-lama*, but, now they were refusing to do the same on account of his client's being a Muslim'. The earlier practice was ordered to be restored.[7]

Alongwith the office the *qanungo*, the family came to posses other financial perquisites over the same area in which they happened to enjoy the rights of *qanugai* as well. A statement of facts submitted by Muhammad Ashiq sometimes in later half of the 18th century records that he was extorting *bhent*, *nānkār* and other imperial gifts out of Devpalpur. He also happened to be the *naib-qanungo* of an area in *nizamat* of the Lownship Biswan and collected the land revenue on behalf of one Tej Singh Gaur.[8] Similarly other *parwana*, issued under the seal of Afzal Khan in AD 1048/AD1638 records that Shaikh Hamid *qanungo* held the responsibilities of *kotwali* in *pargana* Laharpura and was also collecting *sair* taxes from *haveli* Laharpur. But these rights were being usurped by Loqman Chaudhari as theka zakati. The *parwana* set aside latters claim and accepted farmer's representation. In 38th *Ry* of Aurangzeb, Shaikh. Haibatullah, who was the *zamindar* of *tappa* Rosipur executed a *qubuliyat* for some *Khalisa* land in different villages of *pargana* Laharpura and contracted to pay ₹ 27/4 *anna* being the total *jama* of three years i.e. till 1104 F. The *mal-o-wajib* was to be remitted directly to the *fotedor* of the *khālisa-i-sharifa*.

It appears that subsequently the *zamindāri* rights in Laharpur too were acquired by the family or three were combined with the office of the *qanungo*. A *parwana* issued in 1123/1711 recognises these two separate rights of Shaikh Haibat Ullah, he be possessed them from earlier times. The village headman (*muqqadam*), cultivators (*muzāriān*) etc being the *riaya* of that place, were called upon to recognise these two rights of Shaikh Haibat ullah,[9] and he alone was entitled to get all the perquisites attached to *zamindāri* and *qanungo* rights.

The members of the family of *qanungo* sometimes even made recommendations for the imperial favours and subsistence grant to the needy and poor. A *parwana* of

AD 1074/AD 1663 records that Shaikh Muhammad Amin, *qanungo* had brought to the notice of the sublime court the poverty of Shaikh Nazar Muhammad and recommended a subsistance grant for him as a result of which 155 *bighas* of land was assigned to him out of Laharpur as *madad-i-maash.*[10]

There is a very interesting *mahzar* enlisting the services renderd by the ancestors of Shaikh Rahmat Ullah to the cause of religion and social welfare. It also gives us some insight into his relations with the *faujdār* of the area. The exact date of *mahzar* is not given, the text makes a referemce to the 40th RY of Aurangzeb. The petitioner recalls the deeds of his ancestors while they were serving as *qanungo* of the area. They helped the inhabitation of the *qasba* and the building and establishment of the mosque, *madarsa*, *khanqah* and the *sarai*. It is also claimed by the petitioner that due to the efforts of his ancestors the tenets and practices of Islam were established in the locality *juma* and 'Id prayers were held in congregation food was distributed among the poor, arrangements were made for instruction of students and, the *gumashtas* of the *jagirdārs* were well treated, the revenue dues were paid well in time. In the 40th RY of Aurangzeb one Lal Bais of *haveli* Laharpūr had raised the banner of rebellion and indulged in the acts of highway robbery, as a result of these depredations many villages of the *jāgirdār* were desolated. To suppress this uprising, one Muhammad Akram *nāib* of Muhammad Fazil, the Faujdār of Khairabad reached Laharpur and stayed there. He was entertained by the petitioner in befitting manner. But for the reasons best known to him he arrested the petitioner and put him in chains. His plea that his feet be chained (instead of presumably his hands) to enable him offering daily prayers was disregarded. Another questionable act of *nāib faujdār* was that he forceably realized ₹ 5680 from the petitioner inspite of his protests. After much humilation inflicted upon him, he records his release from the confinement as a result of the intervention of some influential persons of the locality.[11] The possibility of his having been punished for any involvement in the revolt of Lal Bais can not be ruled out. However, it is not known to us what action was initated on the basis of this *mahzar*.

The high handeness of the *naib faujdār* made the matters worse for the family, as subsequent *parwāna* of 41st RY of Aurangzeb issued under the seal of Abul Hassan recalls that one Shaikh Sanaullah reported the state of poverty of Shaikh Rahmatullah, who as a result of the letter sent in his favour, was offered services according to his status.[12]

Madad-i-Ma'ash grants

The late 17th century phenomenon of ejecting Hindu grantees to pave the way for the Muslims is also represented. A statement of facts submitted by Muhammad Ashiq *qanungo, pargana* Laharpur records that 77 *bighas* of land from village Kasaila was in *madad-i-maash* grant of one Gulab Rai Khathri since the days of Aurangzeb, but in the last days of that emperor it was resumed and included in *khālisa-i-sharifa* it remained so atleast for the ten years, when his ancestors submitted about the meagre resources and little means of subsistence, hence they were granted the same piece of land in *madad-i-maash*, while even the *zamindari* rights of the same were also given to them. Both were made hereditory. This way 70 years have passed, but now, during the time of Askar Beg Khan *karori*, the heirs of the said family of the Khattris heve started illegal encroachments over the said land.[13] Originally, the family Shaikh Mazhar held the *qanungoi* rights over the 5 *tappās* during the second half of the 16th century but with the passage of time his heirs could manage to get a number of other officer in the same, *tappas*, hence, their perquisites were also raised. From the different areas they realized nānkār, *bhent*, imperial presents, and the urban taxes were also collected by them. Sometimes they acted as *kotwāl*. But the striking feature is that while having such varied resources at their disposal, they tried to get *madad-i-maash* land as well. This was quite contrary to the imperial policy during the 16th century. But as a result of the slackness that had creeped into the Mughal administration in 17th century, such open violations of norms were even ractified.

Caledar of the Documents

LUL 46880 - Farman of Emperor Akbar dated 18 *Rabi* I AH 979/AD 1571. addressed to *Umadatul Mulk* Nizamuddin Muhammad Dost Khan regarding the of Shaikh Mazhar, representation that the villages Danpalpur, Husainpur, Amba and Sultanpur, *pargana* Laharpur, *sarkar* Khairabad were held by him since long. Now, the naib-muqaddam Muhammad Musa, whom the said village i.e. Danpalpur and Husainpur were assigned in lieu of his services is said to be making unnecessary interference. If this is a fact, it is incumbent upon the two parties be summoned before the *sharia't* court and the dispute be settled, after earmarking the taxable land (the grantees) be given possession and no inteference be allowed in this matter.

LUL-46881 - Copy of the proceedings, under the seal of Qazi Muhammad Subhan and Mufti Muhammad Yousuf and other prominent persons of the area dated 21 *Ramzan* AH 1145. The office of the *qanungo* of five tappas in Haveli Lahharpur, Manakapur, Chitamav, Devapalpur and Kharij *pargana* Laharpur, *sarkar* Khairabad, *suba* Awadh, was held by Shaikh Mazhar according to the imperial orders. After his death, the office was recommended by the *diwans* and the *hukkam* of this province for Shaikh Muhammad Amin, to be succeeded by Shaikh Muhammad 'Inayat', after him the office was recommended by the *diwāns* and the *hukkams* for Shaikh Rahmat Ullah, he was succeeded by his real brother Shaikh

Haibat Ullah who continued to hold the said office till date without any inteference or hinderance from any quarter. Attestation of the facts contained in the above proceedings was sought from the people by putting their signatures and affixing the seals.

Five tappas

1. Haveli
2. Mankapur
3. Chitamav
4. Devpalpur
5. Kharij

LUL-46683 **-** *Parwana* addressed to the present and future *mutassadi* of *pargana* Laharpur, *sarkar* Khairabad, dated 5 Rajab AH 1047 says that Shaikh Mubariz represented the matter of kotwali and *sair* were held by Shaikh Hamid *qanungo*, but same had been usurped by Loqman Chaudhary as *theka zakati*. Be it known that after looking into the evidence, the usurpers be restrained and the rights of Shaikh Hamid be restored.

LUL-46885 **-** *Parwana* of Khair Andesh Khan dated 21 Zilhija 25th Ry of Aurangzeb, to the *mutasaaddis* of *parganas* Laharpur. Be it known that the *wakil* of Rahmat Ullah came to the imperial court along with a *parwana* of *umadat-ut-mulk madarul-maham* (Asad Khan?) to the effect that the *qanungoi* of the said *pargana* is held by his client. The grandfather and the father of his client Shaikh Muhammad Amin and Shaikh Inayat Ullah always obtained the signatures of the Chaudharies and the other Hindu *qanungo* on *tumar jama*; but now, contrary to the former practice, they (the chaudharies) and the Hindu *qanungo* are refusing to act accordingly on account of the client's being a Muslim. After examining the *tumārs* and other papers, it is ordered that the earlier practice be adhere to, and nothing be done contrary to it.

LUL-46887 - *Parwana* dated 27 Jamad I AH 1074 addressed to the present and future *'amils* of *pargana* Laharpur, *sarkar* Khairabad. Be it known that since Shaikh Muhammad Amin *qanungo* had recommended that Shaikh Nasar Muhammad had no means for subsistence, therefore, 155 *bighas* of land has been assigned to him out of the said *pargana* as *madad-i-ma'ash*. Order the addresse to deliver the land duly measured and demarcated out of cultivated waste. The grantee was to enjoy all the benefits to busy himself in praying for the perpetuity of the everlasting empire.

LUL-46890 - Copy of *patta-ijara* dated 20 Muharram 38th RY of Aurangzeb under the seal of Muhammad Farooq for the resumed land from village Mirzapur and other villages, *pargana* Laharpur *sarkar* Khairabad. Shaikh Haibat Ullah, the *zamindar* of *tappa* Rosipur has extended a *qubuliyat* for three years w.e.f. *kharif* 1102 F/ to *kharif* 1104 F/ for a total sum of ₹ 27/4 annas. It was incumbent upon him to pay the *mal-o-wajib* (as per details) to the *fotedar* of *Khalisa-i-sharifa*.

4 *chaks* having 135 *bighas*, 10 *biswas*

chak village Mirzapur *chak* village Shahpur

chak villeage Sham Kadar *chak* village Roberkar Khas

92 *bighas*, 18 *bighas* 15 *bighas* 14 *bighas* 1 *beswms*

Jama agreed for three years ₹ 27/4 *annas*

1102F *1103F* *1104F*

₹ 14/4 ₹ 10 ₹ 14

LUL-46891 - *parwana* of Abul Hasan dated 26 Muharram 41 RY of Aurangzeb. Be it known to Shaikh Rahmatullah *qanungo* of *pargana* Laharpur, that his state of poverty has been conveyed by Shaikh Sanaullah. Rest be assured, he should come to this place along with Shaikh Sanaullah and join the service of this well-wisher. He would be treated well and will be offered services according to his status.

LUL-46895 **-** *parwana* of Muhammad Miran dated 19 Zilhij 35th RY of Aurangzeb. Addressed to Shaikh Muhammad Amin *qaungo* of *pargana* Laharpur. Says that details of his situation has been received. It is incumbent upon the addressee that on receipt of this *parwana*, he should report personally to provide some more details. He would be allowed to depart soon, and he should be looked after with care.

LUL-46898 **-** A Statement of the fact having no date presented by Muhammad Ashiq *qanungo*, grandson of Shaikh Qazi, Mufti, *qanungo* and all the residents of *pargana* Laharpur *sarkar* Khairabad. States that 77 bigha land from village Kasaila was held by one Gulab Rae Khattri as *Madad-e-Maash* during the reign of Emperor Aurangzeb, but at the close of his reign the said grant was resumed and was included in *khaliss-sharifa*. It remained so atleast for ten years. Afterwards the governor recommended the name of Shaikh Dost Muhammad for subsistence grant and as per orders of the sublime court, Shaikh was granted the above plot of land by way of *madad-e-m'aāsh* and *zamindāri*. Afterwards, the *'āmil* continued to confirm the said grant issuing the sanads. About 70 years have passed and the land is under the possession of the heirs of the Shaikh. Now, during the karoriship of Askar Beg Khan, some of the descendents of the said Khathri have started illegal encroachments over the said land without any cre-dentials. Requests the addresses in the name of the God to testify to the correctness of the above facts by putting their signatures and affixing their seals.

LUL-46902 **-** Parwana of Abul Qasim dated 10 Ramzan 1123th AH/...........Be it know to the present and future *mutassadis* of *pargana* Laharpur, *sarkar* Khairabad that the office of *qanungo* and *zamindāri* of the said *pargana* were held by Shaikh Haibat Ullah son of Shaikh 'Inayat Ullah since olden times according to imperial *farmāns*. The said rights of the Shaikh are again confirmed, wherefore it is incumbent upon the *muqaddams*, *muzarian* etc. being the *ri'aya* of that place, to recognise the rights of the said Shaikh. The perquisites is attached to these rights were only to be paid to the said Shaikh. The Shaikh was to look after the welfarte of the *ri'aya* and to pray for the long life of the everlasting empire.

LUL-46904 **-** Statement submitted by Muhammad Ashiq seeking attestation to the facts that office of *qanungo* of 5 tappa of *pargana* Laharpur was bestowed upon his ancestor Shaikh Mazhar B. Shaikh Nizam during the reign of emperor Akbar. The title passed on to his son Ghulam Mohiuddin after his death, he was succeeded by his son Muhammad Hamid, then came his son Muhammad Amin, then came Muhammad 'Inayat, then came Rahmat Ullah, then came his brother Haibat Ullah (father of the petitioner), then came Ghulam Rasool (elder brother of the petitioner), finally the petitioner came to enjoy the title. The perquisites of *nānkār* and *bhent* and other imperial gifts were always realized by the ancestors of the petitioner from the area. Similarly, *tappa* Davpalpur has been enlarged by adding a number of adjacent villages; it has been now named as Maharajnagar. Moreover, the petitioner also came to enjoy the naib-*qanungoi* of an area included in the *nizamat* of Biswan. From this region, he realized the land-revenue for one Raja Tej Singh Gaur. The addresses were requested in the name of God to attest the correctness of these facts.

LUL-46905 **-** Attestation is sought on a statement of the facts having no date by Shaikh Rahmat Ullah *qanungo* of *pargana* Laharpur, *sarkar* Khairabad, addressed to the respectable persons and others of the *pargana*. States that the office of *qanungo* of the five tappa of Laharpur is held by petitioner on the basis of inheretence as according to the *farmāns* of the various emperors, ancestors of the petitioner strived to establish the township and the inhabitation of the *qasba*, mosque, *madarsa*, *khanqah* and the rest houses for the travellers were built, the tenants and the practices of Islam were established in the area; *Juma* and '*Idain* prayers were held in congregation, meal was distributed among the poor and destitudes; arrangements were made for the instruction of the students, the *gumashta* of the *jāgirdārs* were well treated and the revenue dues were also paid well in time. Prayer for the perpetuity of the everlasting empire also held continuously, on the Rajab 40th RY of Aurangzeb one Muhammad Akram, *naib-faujdār* of *sarkar* Khairabad arrived along with his forces in *pargana* Laharpur to crush rebellion of Lal Bais, who had started highway robbery and acts of depredation in the area. As a result of his activities, the *jāgirdārs* were unable to realize their salary dues in full. The petitioner attened the camp of *naib-faujdar* in befitting manner, but was later imprisoned by him without any valid reason. His plea that his feet be chained (instead of presumably his hands) to enable him offering daily prayers was disregarded. Another act of the high handedness of the said official was that he forciably took ₹ 5680 from the petitioner inspite of his protests. However, after much humilitations and sufferings, he was set free.

The petition has been attested by seven persons by putting their signatures and affixing the seals.

References

1. A lot of thirty documents was purchased by the library authorities for ₹ 600 from one Mr Ahmad Husain r/o *qasba* Laharpur. these papers have been accessioned in the accession register being serial number from 46878 to 46907.

2. *Ain's* account of the twelve suba finds mention of this pargana. For the modern identification see Irfan Habib, *An Atlas of the Mughal Empire,* OUP, 1982 see sheet number 9A and its notes.
3. The name of the *tappa* occurs in a statement of facts submitted in the court of *qazi* in AH 1145 /AD 1732 See. LUL-46881.
4. LUL-46881 (1145/1732) and TLL - 46904 (n.d.)
5. LUL-46880 (979/1571)
6. LUL-46881 (1145/1732) and TLL - 46904 (n.d.)
7. LUL-46885. It is not clear why at all the *tumar-e-jama*' of one *qanungo* required the authenciation of other *qanungo*?
8. LUL-46904.
9. LUL-46883.
10. LUL-46890.
11. LUL-46902.
12. LUL-46887.
13. LUL-46905.
14. LUL-46898A.

7

Rural Bureaucracy in Cooch Bihar and Assam under the Mughals: Archival Evidence

The Mughals invariably sought to establish an agrarian regime having a centralized structure. The basic information was elicited from the hereditary local officials which was collected by the higher Mughal officials at the provincial level. Such a database was used to formulate agrarian policies further.

It was the interplay of the local know-how and the expertise in handling the ecological and agronomic zones with the Mughal officials, that a long-term policy could evolve in such a manner that its traces are still recognizable in those areas. It is rare to find documentation for the actual process of such evolving of the agrarian policies in different regions, subjugated from time to time.

A study of this process is being attempted here on the basis of twenty-five Mughal documents from 17th-18th centuries at the Department of Historical and Antiquarian Studies, Gawahati, Assam. Photocopies of these documents are available at the National Archives of India, New Delhi, which I have consulted.[1] Most of them are *parwanas* and *saads* issued by the provincial officials from time to time in recognition or confirmation of appointments of the various subordinate officers or their fiscal claims. The bulk of these papers related to family which held the office of the *qanungo* of various *sarkars* for several generations in a fairly large area. These documents also throw light on the nature and magnitude of their perquisites and claims. Important clues are provided about the office of the *chaudhrai* and his claims as well.

Apart from the intrinsic value of these documents the evidence is important enough to enable us examine the quesation whether the Mughal rule was just a passing phase in the history of the region and ended abruptly without leaving any trace of its existence or ushering any change in the structure of economy and society. Certainly, the local records of the region to which these documents pertain, will provide more interesting details about the changes resulting from Mughal occupation and control of Assam and Cooch Behar. A calendar of the documents is appended to this paper.

Office of the *qanungo*

Elsewhere it has been argued that the office of the *sarkar qanungo* was an established feature of the Mughal Empire. It was generally entrusted to some local chieftain or a professional secretarial family of the region. These people were thought to be capable of gleaning the information from each *pargana* because of their caste associations or their ties with the soil.[2] It was only in the 25th R.Y. that Aurangzeb ordered the removal of all the *sarkar* qanungos throughout the empire. Still few exceptions were made to this general rule[3].

Since Mughal rule had yet to gain firm grounds in Cooch Behar and Assam region, it appears, that approval was granted for the appointment of the *sarkar* and *suba qanungo*.

Dastur-i-qanungoi of the one Gabshekhar over '*suba*' Cooch was recognised by the Mughal officials during the reign of Emperor Jahangir. According to a *sanad* issued by Mir Shamsuddin he was entitled to collect ₹ 2 on every ₹ 100 (2% of the total net collection of the *suba*). Taking into account the acts of his fidelity, the officials of the *suba* were directed not to interfere with him in collecting his dues as well as *nankar* (Doc. 15). After the death of Gab Shekhar the office of *khidmat-i qanungo* and *dastur-i nankar* in the four *mahal* falling under the jurisdiction of *sarkar* Kamrup, *sarkar* Dakhin Kol, *sarkar* Dhendri and *sarkar* Bengal Bhoom passed on to Dev Raj, the grandson of Gab Shekhar. The officials, *chaudharis* and *zamindars* of *wilayat* (territory) of Cooch were to recognise him as the permanent *qanungo* of the area in all affairs.

The grantee was to dispatch the papers of *sarishta-i qanungoi* to the office of *diwan* regularly. He was also obliged to strive for the habitation and well being of the *mahals* (Doc. Nos. 20, 22, 24, 12, 14, 1). The twin offices were confereed upon Debi Prasad, the son of Dev Raj after the latter's death. We possess a confirmatory *parwana* issued under the seal of one Saiyid Yusuf. The interesting aspect of this document is that among the addressees we find *qanungos* side by side with the *chaudharis*, *muqqadams* and mutassadis. This forcefully suggests that the family of Gab Shekhar possessed the office of *qanungo* for the entire *wilayat* of Cooch, while separate *qanungos* at the level of *mahal/pargana* were retained (Doc. 17).

It appears that the office of the *naib-qanungo* was also created subsequently, to assist the work of the *sarkar qanungo*. Probably the appointment was made in consent with the principal officer. A *parwana* of the reign of Muhammad Shah instructs the *gumashtas* and the *muharrirs* of the office of the *qanungo* of the area and to receive orders from the appointee for all the work of the *qanungoi*. The incumbent to the newly created office was to keep the staff of the department happy and contented besides adhering to the rules and regulations in discharge of his duties. The appointee was required to provide maintenance to Bulchand, the earlier incumbent on the same post (Doc. 21).

The Mughals often found room for traditionally established local offices and/or nomenclatures in their administration. Hence, we find variations in the nomenclature for the same types of the duties and perquisites throughout the realm. We come across a *parwana* of the last decade of Aurangzeb's reign asking *mutasadis*, *chaudharis* and *muzarian* to recognise one Suraj Chand, *qanungo*–as possessing the post (*khidmat*) of *badkahati* or *badgahati* after the demise of Jagan Nath and Madhu Nand. The appointee was to facilitate the work of collection of *mal* and *sair*, and to work in such a way that the confidence is resposed among the inhabitants of the area, to strive for the increase and well being of the population. The rules of the office were to be adhered to strictly (Doc. 3).

The office of the central *diwan* was always particular about the *mawazina* (revenue collection of previous years, usually ten) paper of each *sarkar* of the empire. In case, these were not received from any part of the kingdom, the *qanungos* were immediately directed to furnish the same. We possess a *dastak* issued to the *qanungos* of *sarkar* Kamrup in A.D. 1671 to the effect that the *mawazina* papers of the *sarkar* for the year A.D. 1076 Bangla/1665 were required, and it was incumbent upon the addressee to dispatch these documents through his knowledgeable *gumatashas*, so that in the central office (*daftar-i-wala*) proper elucidation of the accounts could be done as per rules (Doc. 8).

Perquisites of the Qanungo

Generally the *qanungos* were entitled to 2% of the total collection of the land revenue (*sad-doi*) as their officially sanctioned perquisite. But it seems that many other benefits were also attached to this post. In all probability quite a few offices were combined into one, resulting in a multiplicity of soical perquisities. Gab Shekhar was allotted one *khel*[4] and four *bighas* of land as his *nankar* in *pargana*, Parbhagh yet retaining *saddoi* (2% land revenue) as his *dastur-i qanungoi*. The land in question was not to be assessed (*kharij-az jama*). The grantee was to pray for the well-being of the ever lasting empire, thus, making it similar to *madad-i maash* or-*inam* grant (Doc. 11). The revenues of an entire village, Kurbat, *pargana* Kunwarbhag amounting to ₹ 12 were allotted to Debi Parsad *qanungo* as his *nankar*. the agents of the *jagirdar* of this area were directed not to interfere in the realization of this amount by the agents of the *qanungo* (Doc. 23). An interesting *parwana* in this collection acquaints us with altogether a new form of *mashrut nankar* (conditionan *nankar*). The official of *mahal* Narma, *chakla* Ghora Ghat, *sarkar* Dhenkeri were asked to hand over 50 maunds of cotton to Debi Parsad *qanungo* on the condition that he should strive to increase the income of the government year after year (Doc. 7). It is obvious that the reign being a cotton growing area, the officials were probably unable to collect the revenues; hence, the local man was being encouraged to do it for the authorities.

Since the *qanungos* were not supposed to maintain any armed retainers, they always solicited the support of the government officials in any problem besetting them in realizing their claims. A *parwana* was issued to a high official, Ibn Husain Khan to the effect that since the *zamindars* of *wilayat* Cooch were putting off the payment of the perquisites to Debi Parsad *qanungo* as per representation of his *wakil*, it was incumbent upon the addressee to help him collect the *dastur-i-qanungo* through his *peshkars*. Similarly, he was requested to help in the dispatch of *sarishta-i-qanungoi* to the Central Office (Doc. 18).

Following a representation from Gab Ratan to the effect that the *chaudharis* and *patwaris* of *tappa* Chamaria etc. were withholding the payment of *dastur-i qanungoi* to the petitioner, a *parwana* was issued to another high functionary of the region, Muhammad Murad to ensure the recovery of the arrears after ascertaining the facts from his own *muharrir*. He was to ensure that in future also the petitioner should not encounter any difficulty in realizing his perquisites (Doc. 16).

Office of the Chaudhari

It appears that the office of the *chaudhari* was supposed to be a crucial position in the rural setup, hence, the matters of appointment and continuance were decided upon quite carefully. Fresh appointees were expected to execute personal bonds (*muchalkas*) as well as to furnish agreements (*razinamah*) from the *qanungo* and *riaya* (peasantry). Fortunately, we possess specimens of these papers in the *zimn* of our documents.

In the year 1687 (29th R.Y. of Aurangzeb) the office of the *chaudhari* of *mahal* Kapasnarma, *thana* Rangamati, was transferred from Dharam Raj to Gokul Chand, who incidentally happened to be the *qanungo* of *sarkar Kamrup*. Such an arrangement was made on the recommendations of the *amin* Sad Ullah. The *jama* of the said *mahal* happened to be ₹ 3601. The new incumbent was asked to perform his duties with honesty and deposit the revenue as per agreement (*taahud*) in the royal treasury; he was to desist from collecting illegal cesses. The monthly installment had been fixed in a very uneven manner and according to lunar months seems to be very peculiar feature (Doc. 3). The *qubuliyat* deed executed by the *chaudhari* is reproduced in appendix 'A'.

In another instance we find that the question appointing a *chaudhari* was decided by the officials of the previous functionaries. One Pushapatti *chaudhari* of *pargana* Khorla (only a part), *sarkar* Dhinkeri was dismissed when a complaint was preferred against him. This related to the oppression of the people (*riaya*) of the area, who were now not agreeable to his continuance. The *amin* of the region was left with no choice but to appoint another *chaudhari* for the *paibaqi mahal* (not assigned in *jagir*) of *pargana* Khorla. The new appointee was Bulchand who already happened to be the *chaudhari* of *mahal* (not assigned in *jagir*) of *pargana* Khorla. The new appointee was Bulchand who already happened to be the chaudhari of *mahal* Sair-i Alamganj. Besides executing a *muchalka* promising to keep *riaya* happy and strive for the extension of the cultivation thus, raising the income of the government, the new incumbent furnished a surety bond (*haziri zamini*) executed by a neighbouring *qanungo* taking full responsibility in his behalf. As the previous *chaudhari* had been dismissed on a specific complaint (*nalish*) of the *riaya* and *muqqaddams*, it was thought that in matter of new appointment (Doc. Nos. 5 & 25). Since specimens of such documents are rare, full translations are appended at the end of this section.

The duties of the *chaudhari* are also specified in one of our documents very clearly. The fact that such a narration comes from 1738-39. One Prithi Deb was appointed *chaudhari* of *pargana* Aurangabad known as Senjimadi, *sarkar* Dakhinm kol, *thana* Rangamatti. He was to strive for the increase of the population and extend cultivation. Every single *dam* of the land revenue was to be remitted to the treasury by the end of every fiscal year and in case some amount had not been realized, it was to be paid by the incumbent himself. He was given the sole responsibility in inquiring into acts of theft, robbery and depredations committed within his jurisdiction. The culprits should be awarded punishment, and the lost property was to be restored to the complainant. In case some hidden treasure was discovered, it should be immediately reported to the government. He was to arrange for regular dispatch of *mawazina* papers to the office of the *mutassadi* regularly (Doc. 13).

The information gleaned from these documents is of varied and uneven nature. The documents appear to follow standard forms, but with considerable intrusions of local features. These documents cover fairly a long period from the time of Jahangir to that of Ahmad Shah. This forcefully suggests that in Cooch Behar and western Assam Mughal rule was not a temporary phenomenon, but was fairly well established over the entire period.

Appendix A

(i) *Qubuliyat* deed executed by the *chaudhari*, Gokul Chand in the 29th year of Aurangzeb's reign has been retained in the *zimn* of the *parwana* issued to the concerned officials of *mahal* Kapasnarma, *thana* Rangamatti, etc. has been transferred from Dharam Raj and has been settled upon me. An amount of ₹ 3601 as *jama* with enhancements in the year 1092 Bangla / A.D. 1681 has been agreed upon by me. I undertake to remit the amount to the imperial treasury though installments shown below without hesitation. Therefore, these lines have been committed to writing, as to serve a firm proof for future.

3601 Shahjahani Coins

Principal amount (*asl*)	2800.00
Enhancement (*izafa*)	801.00

Amount of monthly *qist* to be paid to the new incumbent.

Month of *Shawwal* 29th R.Y.	31.00
Month of *Ziqad* 29th R.Y.	41.00
Month of *Zilhiji* 29th R.Y.	51.00

Month of *Muharram* 29th R.Y.	51.00
Month of *Safar* 29th R.Y.	51.00
Month of *Rabi-I* 29th R.Y.	160.00
Month of *Rabi-II* 29th R.Y.	215.00
Month of *Jamada I* 29th R.Y.	225.00
Month of *Jamada II* 29th R.Y.	350.00
Month of *Rajab* 29th R.Y.	501.00
Month of *Shaban* 29th R.Y.	923.00
Month of *Ramzan* 29th R.Y.	1000.00
	3601

(ii)The office of the *chaudhari* of a portion of *pargana* Khorla *sarkar* Dhenkri, a *paibaqi mahal* in *thana* Rangamatti was assigned to Bulchand after the previous incumbent had been dismissed as a result of his oppression (*taaddi*). This time, in order to make the new arrangement foolproof, the following undertakings were obtained by the imperial officials. They are included in the *zimn* of the *parwanas*. They are reproduced in full.

(a) *Machalka* executed on 2nd *Rabi* 17th R.Y. of Aurangzeb. "I, Bulchand, *chaudhari* of a portion of *pargana* (*qismat-i pargana*) Khorla, a *paibaqi mahal* attached tith *thana* Rangamatti have been assigned the *chaudhari* of the said *pargana* following the transfer of Pashupati according to the argreement (*razinamah*) of the *muqqaddams* and the *raiyat* of the said *pargana* which I accepted willingly. I also recognise and promise that I will perform the assigned duties diligently in such a manner that the cultivable land should increase, and that I will not oppress anyone. The peasantry will be kept happy and satisfied by the considerate behaviour. I will pay the stipulated revenues of the government every year in time. If any amount remained unpaid, I will be personally responsible for the same. I will collect the perquisites (*marasim*) strictly as per regulations. These things have been put into writing to serve as record whenever needed in future."

(b) The *razinamah* (deed of consent) submitted by the *riaya* (peasantry) of *pargana* Khorla on 22nd *Safar* 7th R.Y of Aurangzeb: "We the peasants of *pargana* Khorla, *mahal-i-paibaqi* of *sarkar* Dhinkri, *thana* Rangamatti state that we were being ruined due to the oppressions of Pashupati. Therefore, quite willingly and totally on our own accord we accept (the appointment) Bulchand for which Suraj Chand *qanungo* has furnished surety (*hazir-zamin*) on his behalf. We undertake that, when he obtains the *sanad* of *chaudhari*, we will pay the revenue as before. therefore, this *sanad* of *razinamah* is written so that it may serve as record whenever required in future."

(c) The *hazir zamini* (surety bond for presenting) executed on 7th *Rajab*, 7th R.Y. of Aurangzeb. "I Suraj Chand *qanungo*, *sarkar* Kamrup etc. say that the *khidmat-i chaudhari* of a portion of *pargana* Khorla, a *mahal-i paibaqi* of *sarkar* Dhenkri, *thana* Rangamatti, *suba jannat-ul bilad* Bangala, has been in assignment of Bulchand as per *sanad* of Mir Rafi-Ullah. I have stood as a surety (*hazirzamini*) for the appointee to present him for depositing the land revenue of the part of the *pargana* in the treasury. In case he absents himself I undertake to bring him back, in case it is not possible, then I myself will undertake the responsibility of the *pargana*. Therefore, this *hazir zamini* is written, so that it may serve as record whenever required in future."

Appendix B

(The calendar of the documents has been arranged in chronological sequence).

1. **A.H. 1023 (sic)/A.D. 1614:** *Parwana* to the officials of *suba* Cooch directing them to recognise the *dastur-i qanungoi* of Gab Shekhar (amounting to 2% of the land revenue) which the appointee held on basis of a *sanad* issued by Mir Shamsuddin. The appointee was also entitled to claim his *nankar* from the area (2551/15).

2. **A.H. 1029 (sic)/A.D. 1620:** *Ruqa* to Gab Ratan *qanungo*–Acknowledges the receipt of his *arzdasht* and assures for the imperial favours. Copy of the same has been dispatched to Saiyid Firoz along with the instructions to which he should adhere. The addressee is asked to help the collection of *mal-i wajibi* well in time, besides keeping the people happy and strive for the increase in cultivation (2551/19).

3. **A.H. 1035 /A.D. 1626:** *Parwana* to the officials, *chaudharis* and *patwaris* of *pargana* Parbhag, (*suba* Cooch) to the effect that one *khet* and 4 *bighas* of land as *nankar* alongwith *dastur-i qanungoi* of two rupees on every hundred have been confirmed in favour of Gab Shekhar, *qanungo*. The land (in grant) was to remain as *kharij-az jama*. The addresses were to maintain regularity in paying of his *dastur* (2551/11).

4. **A.H. 1064/A.D. 1654:** Official letter to Muhammad Murad intimating him tht according to the petition of Gab Ratan *qanungo*, the *chaudharis* and *patwaris* of *tappa* Chamaria were with holding the payment of *dastur-i qanungoi*. The addressee was urged to facilitate the collection of the arrears and ensure the regular payment after ascertaining the facts from his own *muharrirs* (1551/16).

5. **A.H. 1075/A.D. 1664:** *Parwana* to the officials, *chaudharis* and *qanungos*, *pargana* Khorla, *sarkar* Dhenkri, *thana* Rangamatti intimating the appointment of Bulchand as *chaudhari* of a part of *pargana* Khorla, after affecting the dismissal of Pashupati, with whom the people were unhappy on account of his reported oppressions (2551/5).

6. **A.H. 1075/A.D. 1664:** *Sanad* to the officials, *qanungos*, peasants and other of *pargana* Khorla, *sarkar* Dhenkri, *thana* Rangamatti intimating the appointment of Bulchand as *chaudhari* of a part of *pargana* Khorla, as per orders of Mir Rafi Ullah, the *amin* of *sarkar* Dhenkri. Further, it is clarified that the appointment has been made after getting a surety bond (*razinamah*) from Suraj Chand, *qanungo* of *sarkar* Kamrup. Contains the usual recitations about the duties and functions (1551/25).

7. **A.H. 1076/A.D. 1666:** *Parwana* to the officials, *chaudharis* and *zamindars* of *wilayat* Cooch intimating them the appointment of Dev Raj grandson of Gab Shekhar as *qanungo* of the area on consideration of his loyalty and fidelity with the usual; *dastur-i qanungo* and *nankar*. Besides listing the usual duties of the appointee he was specifically asked to submit the *sarishta-i-qanungoi* in the office as per customs (2551/20).

8. **A.H. 1076/A.D. 1666:** *Parwana* to the officials, *chaudharis* and the *zamindars* of *wilayat* Cooch intimating about the same appointment as of above (1551/22).

9. **A.H. 1078/A.D. 1667:** *Parwana* issued to the officials, *chaudharis*, *qanungos*, *muqqadams* and *riaya* of *sarkar* Kamrup *wilayat* Cooch Hajo intimating about the confirment of *dastur-i qanungoi* and *nankar* in favour of Debi Parsad, son of Dev Raj. Instructs the addressees

to pay these perquisites of the appointee regularly (2551/17).

10. **A.H. 1081/A.D. 1671:** *Dastak* to the *qanungos* of sarkar Kamrup directing them to send *mawazina* papers of the said *sarkar* upto the year 1076 *Bangala* (1669) forthwith. This should be sent through their knowledgeable *gumashtas* to the *daftar-i wala* for reconciliation of the accounts (2551/8).

11. **A.H. 1092/A.D. 1681:** *Parwana* to the officials, *chaudharis*, and *zamindar* of *sarkar* Kamrup etc. *wilayat* Cooch intimating them about the renewal of the office of *qanungoi* in favour of Debi Parsad. Recitation is made regarding the well known duties of the appointee (2551/24).

12. **A.H. 1076/A.D. 1666:** *Parwana* to the *chaudharis* of *pargana* Baharband and Bari intimating about the confirmation of the *qanungoi* rights of Debi Parsad through a separate order. It is, there-fore, recorded that with effect from A.H. 1087/A.D. 1676 the *dastur-i qanungoi* of the incumbent are recognised and he was supposed to provide the sarishta paper from that year (2551/14).

13. **A.H. 1092/A.D. 1681:** *Parwana* to the *gumashtas* of *jagirdars* of *pargana Kunwarbhag*, *sarkar* Kamrup informing them about the fact that the agent of Debi Parsad *qanungo* has petitioned that village Kart having a *jama* of ₹ 12 has been in assignment of his patron by way of *nankar*. Therefore, it was incumbent upon the addressees to recognise the said village as such (2551/23).

14. **A.H. 1092/A.D. 1681:** *Takid* to a high official .... Khan to the effect that the *wakil* of Debi Parsad *qanungo* of

wilayat Cooch has petitioned that the *zamindars* of the region are putting off the payment of the *dastur-i qanungoi* due from them. The addressee was urged to ask his *peshkars* to collect the same from the erring *zamindars* and deliver it to the said *qanungo*. Also the *qanungo* should be directed to send the *sarishta* papers soon (2551/18).

15. **A.H. 1093/A.D. 1682:** *Parwana* to the officials of Narma *chakla* Kunta Ghat, *sarkar* Dhenkri informing them about the grant of fifty mounds of cotton (*kapas*) *nankar* to Debi Parsad *qanungo* of the area on the condition that he should strive to increase the income of the government every year 2551/7).

16. **A.H. 1097/A.D. 1685:** *Parwana* addressed to the official of certain *pargana*. Since the text is badly mutilated at the left hand margin leaving vital gaps at the end of every line, hence, the calendar has not been attempted (2551/4) (₹ 301 *jama* of entire village have been assigned).

17. **A.H. 1098/A.D. 1687:** *Parwana* to the officials of *Kapasnarma thana* Rangamatti informing them about the appointment of Gokul Chand *qanungo* of *sarkar* Kamrup as the *chaudhari* of above *mahal*; on the recommendations of Sad Ullah, the *amin*. This *mahal* had an annual *jama* of ₹ 3601 from the beginning of 1092 Bangala/AD 1681-82. Directs the addressees to recognise the appointee as such. Recitation is made regarding the duties and functions of the *chaudhari*. The *zimn* contains monthly breakup (*qist*) of the annual *jama* to be paid by the new incumbent (2551/2).

18. **81 Julus/A.D. 1688:** *Parwana* to the officials, *chaudharis*, and *zamindars* of *wilayat* Cooch, intimating them about the confirmation of *qanungoi* of the area in

favour of Debi Parsad. the appointee was entitled to claim the *dastur-i qanungoi* and *nankar* as before. Usual recitation about his duties (2551/1).

19. **41 Julus/A.D. 1697:** *Parwana* to the *muqqadams*, *chaudharis*, *qanungo*, *riaya* and *muzar-i*, *pargana* Kunwarbhag etc. *sarkar* Kamrup informing them about the grant of the office of *badghahat* of these *parganas* to Suraj Chand, the *qanungo*. Directs the addressees to recognise the appointee as the permanent *badgahat* of the area. Details of his duties are also provided (2551/3).

20. **1144 Bangala/A.D. 1738:** *Parwana* to the *gumashtas* and *muharrirs* of the office of *qanungo*, *sarkar* Dhenkri, *thana* Rangamatti intimating them about the appointment of Bishan Chand as the *naib-qanungo* of the area on behalf of Bul Chand, *qanungo*. Instructions to the appointee and addressees about the duties and perquisites etc. (2551/21).

21. **A.H. 1163/A.D. 1750:** *Parwana* to Har Gopal on his appointment as *qanungo pargana* Baharband, *sarkar* Bangal Bhum after the demise of his father late Ram Gopal. Besides general duties, the appointee was asked to attest the *pargana* papers carefully and keep the *sarishta* ready to dispatch every year (2551/6)

22. **A.H. 1166/A.D. 1754:** Sanad to the *qanungo*, *riaya*, *muzaris* and inhabitants of pargana Aurangabad alias Sangiumari, *sarkar* Dhenkri, *thana* Rangamatti, *suba* Bengal informing them about the appointment of Durga Parsad as the *zamindar* of the said *pargana* with usual *nankar*. The incumbent was to collect the *mal-i wajib* and remit it to the royal treasury every month. The addressees were asked to recognise him as the only *zamindar* of the area (2551/9).

The last document of the collection pertains to the period of East India Company, hence, no calendar is offerred here.

References

1. All these photocopies are bounded together, and have been acessioned in the Accession Register (Oriental Records Division) National Archives of India at serial no. 2551. However, for easy reference each document has been assigned a sub-number running from 2551/1 to 2551/25.
2. For example, the office of *sarkar qanungo* of *sarkar* Chanderi, *suba* Malwa ran in the family of one Mathura Das and his descendants for a very long period in hereditary succession. The documents of this family have survived the ravages of the time and have been studied by me in, "The *Sarkar Qanungo*: 16th-17th Century Documents." Proceedings of Indian History Congress (1985) Amritsar Session, pp. 253-264. [chapter of the book]
3. This Important measure of Aurangzeb has been mentioned very briefly by Saqi Mustaid Khan, *Maasir-i-Alamgiri*, Bib. Indi. Kolkata, 1870-73, pp. 190-1. However, a *hasbul-hukm* of Asad Khan issued in 1683 described this measure in great details. For full translation of the text as well as *zimn* see my paper, op. cit., pp. 262-3. [pp. of the book].
4. A unit of agricultural land which was considered equal to sixty *bighas* especially in Bengal.

Document No. 4. A *Qubuliyat* deed executed by Chaudhury Gokul Chand for the year AD1681. He promises to pay an amount of Rs.3601 as *jama* [including the inhancement] in the twelve monthly instalments. The *jagir* was transferred to him from Dharamraj on the complaint by the peasants.

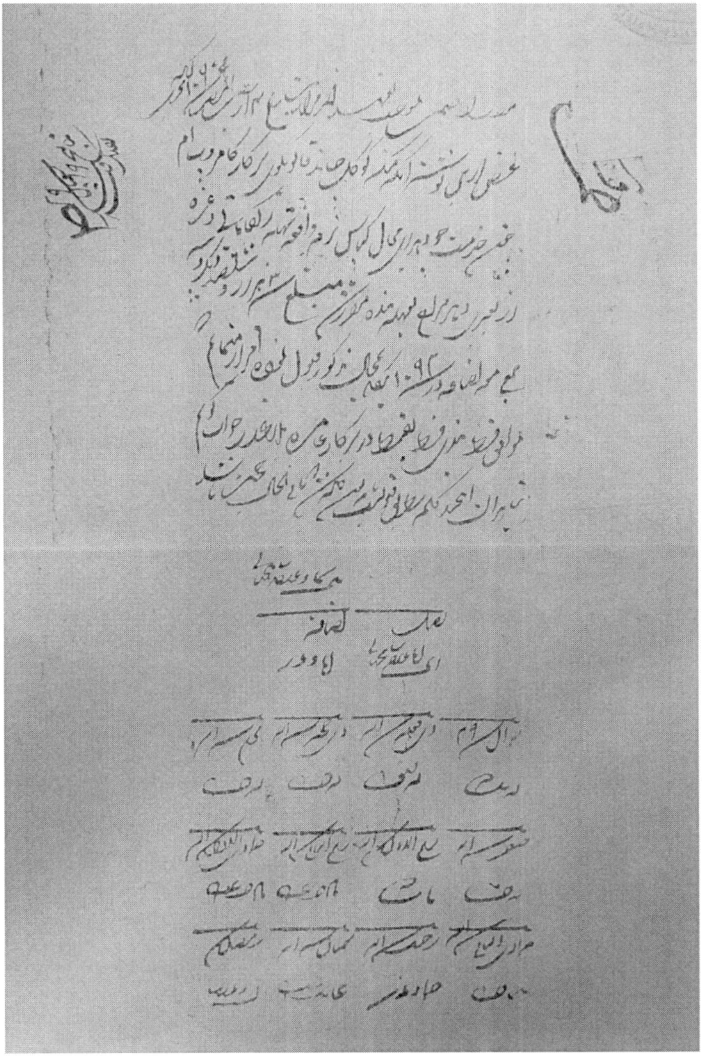

Document No. 5. Fascimile of the *muchalka* executed by Bulchand Chaudhury [in the RY 17th of Aurangzeb] of Pargana Khorla, thana Rangamati in Cooch Bihar. He accepts to perform all the duties as per agreement of the *muqaddams* and chaudhuries of the area.

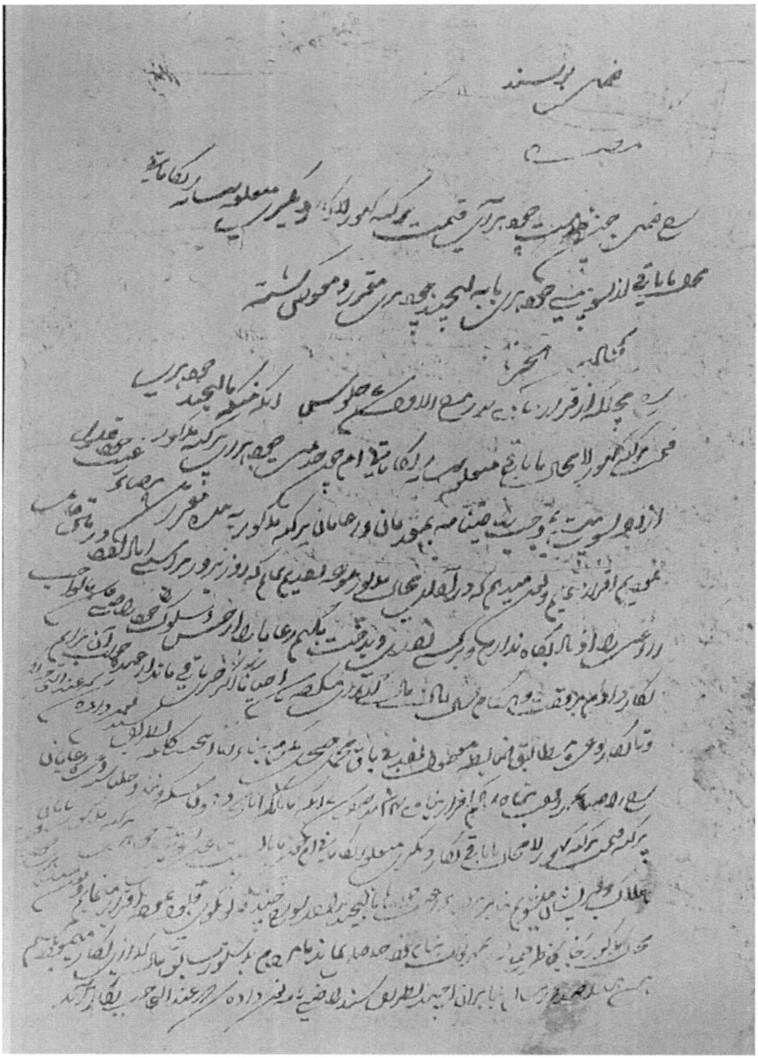

Document No. 6. *Parwana* to the *Gomashtas* [agents] and *muharrirs* [scribes] in the office of Qanungo, Sarkar Dhenkri, thana Rangamati, issued in the year AD1738 intimating them the appointment of kishenchand as the naib Qanungo of the area

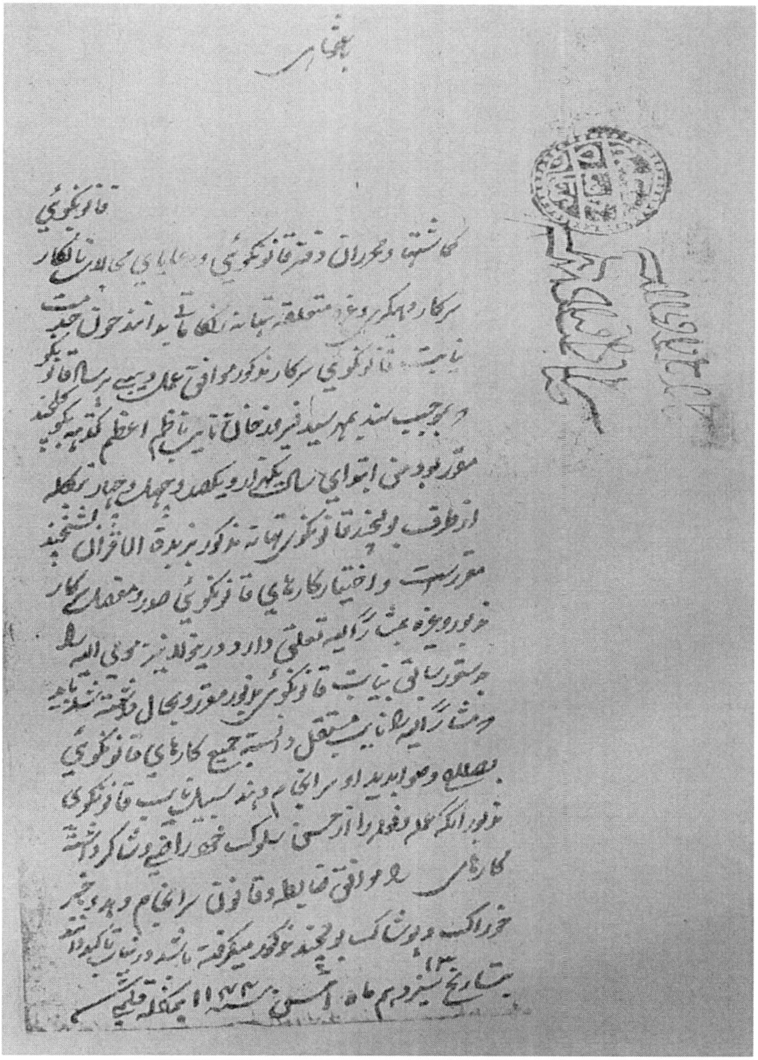

Revenue Grants: Family of Grantees and State

8

Tension and Conflicts in the Agrarian Society of Awadh: A Study of Revenue Grantees

The *madad-i ma'āsh* holders formed a minor segment of the agrarian society of Awadh during the Mughal period, but their conditions are illuminated by an extensive documentation. There appear to have been substantial conditions with these grants, in the beginning; later on these were dropped altogether and the grantees themselves were elevated to the status of the 'Army of the Prayer'. Still, we find that the successive Mughal rulers insisted on confirmatory orders after the death of the original grantees. In matters of inheritance to grants the rules of *shari'at* were not applicable as *madad-i ma 'ash* was supposedly an article of loan *('ariyat)*.

At the same time we find that several of the state functionaries, particularly the ecclesiastical officers were holders of revenue-grants in lieu of their pay claims. Most of these grants were concentrated in particular villages. Often the induction of these outsiders as co-sharers of the social surplus in the agrarian society was resented by the *zamindar*. But their 'reservations' mostly related to trivial matters, which could be solved by the local officials.

An attempt is made here to examine some fresh evidence of the tension and conflicts between the revenue-grantee and the *zamindar* as well as the elements of co-operation between the two classes.

The clashes mainly occurred between the grantees with some position in the official hierarchy and the rural elite. It is necessary to study the nature of the jurisdiction of these grantees as officials. We may take up as an illustration the fortunes of a single family, where documents have survived. This family was established at *pargana* Sandila, *sarkar* Lucknow, since the heyday of the Delhi Sultanat. It enjoyed *madad-i ma 'dsh* grants in lieu of its members rendering many ecclesiastical duties like *qaza, ihtisab* and *nirkhnawis,* etc.

The Context of Clashes

The association of the *zamindari* rights with domination of a particular caste in a *pargana* had been the most peculiar feature of the agrarian life in Awadh during the Mughal period. Any attempt to disturb this caste hegemony often resulted in an open clash between the local officials and the members of the affected castes. Since the genesis of these conflicts lay in the distribution of social surplus, the conflict often cut across religious lines.

A perusal of the *suyurghal* statistics in the *Ain-i Akbari's* account of the 'Twelve *subas*' shows that in absolute terms the number of persons holding *madad-i ma'āsh* rights in *parganas* with Rajput and other non-Muslim *zamindars* was larger than those holding these rights in the *pargana* having Muslim *zamindars.* An analysis of the data leads us to some interesting conclusions. In the five *parganas* of the various *sarkar* of *suba* Awadh where the *zamindars* happened to be Muslims, the percentage of total *naqdi* (cash) alienated by way of *suyurghal* ranged from 0.49 per cent *(pargana* Utraula', *sarkar* Gorakhpur) to 12.6 per cent *(pargana* Unam, *sarkar* Lucknow), while *pargana* Ibrahimabad, *sarkar* Lucknow by way of an exception records a high percentage i.e. 23.3 per cent of the total *naqdi.*

In the other six *parganas* where Muslims are the co-sharers of *zamindari* rights with the Rajputs, the *jama'* alienated by way of *suyurghal* ranges from 1.78 per cent *(pargana* Manwi, *sarkar* Lucknow) to 18.49 per cent *(pargana* Sidhaur, *sarkar* Lucknow). While in another 72 *pargana* with no Muslim *zamindari* these grants constituted between 0:03 per cent *(pargana,* Dariyapara, *sarkar* Gorakhpur) and 18.74 per cent *(pargana* Sihali, *sarkar* Lucknow) of the total *naqdi*. The remaining 47 *parganas* recorded no *suyurghal* grants at all. This included *pargana* Anona, *sarkar* Awadh, where the *zamindars* were Chauhan Rajputs, newly converted to Islam. In Awadh, at least, the grantees appear to have been indifferent to the community of the *zamindars* while seeking grants.[1]

In any case, the total amount of the *jama* 'alienated through such grants in 1598 was only 5.72 per cent of the total *naqdi* in *suba* Awadh. But the fact that the *madad-i ma 'ash* grants as a rule were made out of the cultivable waste with the implicit purpose of making it cultivable; the standard formula used invariably in such orders was, *zamin-i uftada-laiq- i ziraat kharij-az jama';* at the most 1/3 of the total area and at the later stages ½ of the total grant was out of the cultivated land *(mazru)*.[2] It is to be remembered that the *suyurghal* figures of the *Ain-i Akbari* represent only the loss of revenue to the state through such alienations, and not the actual income from *madad-i ma 'ash* lands. It might have included the amount distributed through cash allowances, but this is not clear. Holders of the *madad-i ma 'āsh* rights *per se* posed no threat to the dominant elite of the area, neither could they ever claim any fiscal perquisites belonging to the *zamindar.*[3] The resistance to the induction of the grantees from outside by the local elements generally centered around questions like not relinquishing the cultivated land or, in *zortalab* areas, refusal by the *peasants/ zamindars* to pay the land-revenue. A quick redressal of these matters even by the local officials could greatly relieve the grantees. Often a change in the area of grant was made in the same village or *pargana* under the usual administrative procedures. So the acquisition and possession of the prime land in the village and insistence on an uninterrupted flow of the revenues to the grantees was a major factor of tension, but it was kept at the manageable limits. Such question could have seldom caused any major law-and-order problem.

But things assumed alarming dimensions when these revenue grantees happened to be the holders of ecclesiastical offices as well. Since such officers had a close proximity to the officials at the Centre and they had to perform many unpopular duties in the region, they could become easy targets of recalcitrant *zamindars*. These *zamindars* often thought of expelling such people from the area of their control.

A statement of the facts presented by the *qazi* family in the *faujdari* jurisdiction of Baiswara in the year AD 1662 sets the context of conflict quite unambiguously. It describes the situation obtaining there as follows:

> the region of Baiswara happens to be the abode of infidelity, and all the twenty-one *parganas* are the home of refuge of the Bais people. Out of these, six *parganas* have *qazis,* whereas fifteen *parganas* have neither *qazis* nor mosques, nor do arrangements exist either for the *azan* or for the congregational prayers. The fact that the ancestors of this family of the *qazi* had supposedly exercised jurisdiction over all the twenty-one *parganas* earlier, and there had been on going clashes between them and the Bais Rajputs, this way eighty years had passed and consequently the *qazis* lost their jurisdiction *(amal)* from 15 *parganas*. None has cared so far to eradicate the sources of infidelity; therefore, the petitioner, Qazi Maudud, deemed it necessary to report the matter to the Emperor Aurangzeb."[4]

Not only the holders of the ecclesiastical offices were subjected to the *zamindar's* wrath, but also the peasants residing in the villages of their *madad-i ma 'ash* were terrorised by the tumultous *zamindars* when they were out to settle scores with these officers. Cattle, prized possession of the peasantry, often attracted them, and villages were raided to lift livestock.

A petition from the family of the *qazi* from *pargana* Parsadepur in the year AH 1061 /AD 1652 complains of the raid in their *madad-i ma 'ash* villages by the Kanhpuria Rajputs of *pargana* Salon:

> they raided the *madad-i ma 'ash* villages of the petitioners with a large number of their clansmen and carried away 940 oxen and buffaloes from the villages of Saleempur and Nizampur. This act was committed without there being any justification and with such impunity that, "they wounded even those two persons who had informed the Emperor of their misdeeds. The infidels are perpetuating such acts of oppression against the Muslims."[5]

The examples of such clashes could be multiplied, but it should not be assumed that the grantees holding ecclesiastical offices could be dislodged in this way from any region. They got protection from the Emperor in case of such clashes. There are instances, too numerous to be cited, when imperial *farmans* were issued to award exemplary punishments to the guilty in case of any loss sustained by the grantees.

One is naturally tempted to know about the actual working of the office of the *qazi* and other related offices in rural life, as to establish what duties they performed which brought them or had the potential of directly involving them in tussles with the *zamindar* of the area. The following relates to a case study of the establishment of a *qazi* family at Sandila, presently in Hardoi District of Uttar Pradesh.

The Office of the Qazi and rural Society

A series of documents in the acquired collection of the National Archives of India enables us to study the ecclesiastical offices and the land grants held by the descendants of famous

Chishti mystic Shaikh Fariduddin Ganj Shakar (d. 1265). The founder of this branch settled at *pargana* Sandila *sarkar* Lucknow, was one Shaikh 'Ali Lahori, who was said to have been the grandson of the celebrated saint. He settled here, towards the close of the thirteenth century and was appointed the *qazi* of *shiqq* Sandila. The revenues of village Dhakua were assigned to him as *wazifa,* while other fiscal imposts, Iike *wujuhat* and *awarizat* of the village were assigned to him to meet the expenses for the occasion of the *'Urs* of the celebrated saint.[6] Thus, we have here an example of a grant made for a specific purpose, rather than a personal grant.

The members of this family continued to hold the office of the *qazi* with many additional duties, and enjoyed fiscal perquisites attached thereto. The geneological chart showing the names and indicating their approximate tenure as the *qazi* of the *pargana* Sandila, has been worked out by Mr Zakir Husain showing the continuance of the family down to the annexation of the kingdom of Awadh. The table spans over a period of about 600 years, but we stand on surer grounds with the accession of Akbar. As the family records are varied in nature, dealing with the working of the quasi-religious institution at the local level and the various problems encountered by them. Often their remunerations and perquisites were in jeopardy thus, making them a vulnerable target of the *zamindars'* manipulations. This way they became more openly inclined towards the official side rather than identifying themselves with the local elements.

Documents from the reign of Akbar make one presume that Qazi Nasrullah held the office of the *qazi* and *muhtasib* of *pargana* Sandila and its environs. These offices passed on to successive generations. In remuneration for their discharging the duties, a number of villages and other land grants by way of *madad-i ma 'āsh* were made over to them. Still other grants were also given either on account of some public benefits which arose there from or as absolutely unconditional and unrelated to any obligation.[8]

The office of the *muhtasib* (censor of morals) and *nirkh nawis* (price-reporter) appear attached to the office of the *qazi,* also in the *farman* of Aurangzeb issued in favour of Shaikh 'Imaduddin on 11th *Rajab* 1091/A.D.1680. The duties connected with these offices too have been listed. These included:

> the delivering of judgements in matters of disputes and distribution of the (legal shares among the heirs of the deceased, attestation of the *chaknama* (demarcation papers) and other documents of legal nature, inducing the people to offer the (prescribed) prayers and to follow the religious injunctions, award of punishments, holding of the Friday and other congregational prayers, keeping an eye over the drunkards, miscreants and other bad characters; fixing the prices of essential commodities, standardisation of the weights and measures, and dispatching the *roznamcha* (daily reports) containing a summary of the prices to the (imperial court).[9]

Land-grants held by the members of the family reveal some interesting features. Qazi 'Imaduddin held an annual *wazifa* of ₹ 270, but sometimes afterwards the cash-grant was converted into a land-grant, and village Maner, *pargana* Sandila, with a total *jama'* of ₹ 203 was assigned to him by way of *madad-i ma'ash* grant. This grant was confirmed on 13th *Safar* 14th RY/AD 1671.[10] The previous officials *(mutassadi) of the jagirdar* and *khalisa-i sharifa* had in addition made over the revenues of the villages Siyamao and Maner, *pargana* Sandila, to Shaikh 'Imaduddin. This was confirmed by a *parwana* of 16th *Rabi*/16th R.Y./A.H.1084/A.D. 1673. Again, we find him receiving 200 *bighas* as *madad-i ma 'ash* from village Mahsona. But in case of this grant a condition was imposed that the grantee was to continue in service *(khidmat)* and was not to realise taxes like *mehrana* and *nikahana.*[12] Another *sanad* of 15th *Shawwal* 22nd R.Y./AD1680 states that Qazi

'Imaduddin had been assigned the revenue of a village having the *jama' kamil* (maximum assessment) of ₹ 200 to ₹ 250. This grant too was made in lieu of service.[13] In the 39th R.Y./ AD1697, the revenues of village Khajari having total *jama'* of ₹ 440 and the village Dhakua having a *jama'* of ₹ 5, were assigned to Qazi 'Imaduddin as *madad-i ma'ash.* From yet in another *parwana* regarding village Mirzapur, *pargana* Sandila included in the *madad-i ma'ash* grant of *Qazi* 'Imaduddin, the revenues of this village are said to have been misappropriated by others illegally, so that it had to be restored to him and an enquiry was ordered.[14] In AH1095/AD1684, the revenues of village Maini *pargana* Sandila amounting to ₹ 270 annually were assigned to Qazi 'Imaduddin as *tankhwah* (salary).[15] This was possibly a temporary assignment.

These grants were made to the Qazi for fulfilling duties of his office. But he seems to have obtained further concessions by claiming to use his land for public benefit. In 1670 he was granted a plot of 8 *bighas* of uncultivated *(banjar)* land in the vicinity of *qasba* Sandila in order to raise a garden or orchard, "for the welfare of the general public."[16] Again on 19th *Ramzan* 21st R.Y./AD1679, he was granted 10 *bighas* again in Sandila for the purpose of raising there an orchard, digging wells, and planting trees alongside the highway for the rest and relief of travellers and destitutes.[17] Interestingly enough such arrangements were resented by the owners *(malikan)* of the land (probably the *zamindar)* and hence, the grantee had to request for the transfer of his grant elsewhere.[18] This was done with an increase of 7 *bighas* land, but with the additional obligation of establishing a mosque and *khanqah.* Fortunately, we possess the *chaknama* deed for the demarcation of these 17 *bighas.*[19]

A *parwana* issued in the 18th RY/AD1675 confirms a land grant of 294 *bighas* held by Qazi 'Imaduddin in *pargana* Nimkhar, *sarkar* Khairabad. This grant was designed to cover the expenses incurred by the grantee in feeding poor scholars and other destitutes at his *khanqah.*[20] The reference to *khanqah* confirms the mystic predilections of the *qazi,* who otherwise should have been an orthodox jurist. Similarly in 24th RY/ AD1682 he obtained the revenue-free grant of village Mairat, *pargana* Nimkhar, *sarkar* Khairabad. This grant too was made by way of grant for same purpose.[21] Apparently, this family in the seventeenth century confined itself to income from grants and did not acquire *zamindari* rights of any sort.

The clashes between the revenue grantees and the superior fiscal right holders were mainly to control the flow of surplus and the prime land in the village. In no way could these clashes be termed as 'local battles between Hindus and Muslims' or 'the communal land wars'.[22] In fact we have seen that invariably the change in the area of grant was made within the same village and such arrangements were seldom opposed by the *zamindar.* One should also remember that such situations were confined to certain areas, the very regions which have acquired considerable notoriety for the recalcitrant attitude of their *zamindar.*[23]

APPENDIX A

Table 1: *Sarkar* wise Break up of the *Suyurgahal* Statistics of *parganas* having Muslim *zamindari*

I	*II*	*III*	
No. of the parganas	***Total jama (dams)***	***Suyurghal (dams)***	***% III as to II***
4	(a) *Sarkar* Awadh 45,00,922	3,06,288	6.8%
1	(b) *Sarkar* Gorakhpur 13,97,367	6,935	0.49%
	(c) *Sarkar* Bahraich (No *pargana* with Muslim *zamindars)*		
	(d) *Sarkar* Khairabad (same as in C)		
7	(e) *Sarkar* Lucknow 1,75,84,829	17,40,280	9.89%
12	**2,34,83,118**	**20, 53,503**	**8.74%**

Table 2: *Sarkar* wise Break up of the *Suyurghal* Statistics of *parganas* without Muslim *zamindari*

16	(a) *Sarkar* Awadh		
	3,63,37,212	13,77,877	3.79%
5	(b) *Sarkar* Gorakhpur		
	52,56,242	99,280	0.80%
5	(c) *Sarkar* Bahraich		
	2,02,42,182	1,06,482	5.24%
	(d) *Sarkar* Khairabad		
	39,41,541	16,56,100	4.15%
29	(e) *Sarkar* Lucknow		
	5,34,54,089	28,74,330	5%
71	**11,92,31,266**	**61,14,069**	**5.44%**

References

1. See Appendix 'A' for the tables. The figures of the tables are based on the two Mss. of *Ain-i Akbari,* Br. Museum Add, 5645 and Add 6552.
2. Irfan Habib, *Agrarian System of Mughal India,* p. 302 and notes.
3. It was only with the increasing monotization of the proprietary rights during the 17th century that the grantees could purchase such rights and could become *ijaradars. In pargana* Hisampur, *sarkar* Bahraich, see the example of Saiyid Muhammad Arif, who was originally a revenue grantee, and made a considerable fortune. (lrfan Habib, *op. cit.,* pp. 150-52).
4. *NAI-2618/6.* This representation has as many as six seals of high officials, two of them of the *jagirdar.* It uses the word *ta'alluqa,* which appears to be the earliest reference to this institution in the proper context. Apart from this, topographical details have also been provided. The length of the *faujdari* of Baiswara *nizamat* in the east-west direction between *pargana* Dalmau and Harha was 25 *karoh,* the width in the south-north, lying between river Ganges and the bank of Sai river, was 15 *krohs.* Also the names of all six *parganas* under the jurisdiction of the *qazis* as well as of the 15 *parganas* from where they have been expelled are given.
5. Abdul Qadir Collection No. 4, U.P. State Archives, Lucknow. This petition has 7 seals three of them of the *jagirdar* of the area; and 14 signatures (5 of them in Devanagiri script). It is dated 3rd *Jamad* AH 1061/A.D.1652

6. Any textual references to this branch are not forthcoming from the sources. Similarly the documents relating to Shaikh Ali Lahori have not survived the ravages of time. However, Mr. Zakir Husain has been able to study the early fortunes of this family during the Turco-Afghan period. See 'Some Original Tughlaq Documents and their Significance. *PIHC* (1989) pp. 219-29. A cursory account of this family has been given by Raja Durga Prasad, *Tarikh-e Sandila,* (Urdu) Lucknow, 1915, pp. 266-68.
7. Zakir Husain, *op. cit.,* p. 221.
8. *NAI-1386* (974 AH/1566 AD). This *hukm* (order) was issued to confirm the earlier imperial grant of 60 *bighas* of *madad-i ma'ash* land in village Khanjaura, *qasba* Sandila, in favour of Qazi Nasrullah and Qazi Mubarak. It was asserted that the grantees were to be treated as the *jagirdar* of the area.(?) *(NAI-1585).*

   A significant circular issued by Shaikh Abdul Nabi (though undated, but datable from the fact that it was issued after Shaikh had performed *haj)* records the facts of the division of the *madad-* i *ma'āsh* land in the family of the *qazi* which was again transferred to the main line after the death of other co-sharers without any heir. For other citations in favour of Qazi Nasrullah, *See NAI-1255.*

   The *madad-i ma 'āsh* grants attached with the office of the *qazi* continued to increase. A *parwana* (AH1081/A.D.1670) records 200 *bighas* in village Todakpur and 100 *bighas* in village Kasmandi, *pargana* Sandila in favour of *Qazi* 'Imaduddin, (NAl-1382).
9. *NAI-1434* (1091/AD1681) After Qazi 'Imaduddin, one Ahmad Beg was appointed *Qazi.* His connection with 'Imaduddin's family is not established. He was for some reason removed. and a *farman* was issued on 6th Rajab 44th RY/AD1700 conferring the office of the *qazi* on one Sharafuddin, son of 'Imaduddin with 100 *bighas* as *madad-i ma 'āsh* on the condition of the service and non-realisation of the dues as *mehrana* and *nikahana.* See NAl-1385 (1112/1700).
10. *NAI-1381. The jama'* was less than the cash grant, perhaps what is to be expected, since the grantee could in time raise the revenue through the extension of cultivation.
11. *NAI-1271*
12. *NAI-1273*
13. *NAI-1374*
14. *NAI-1274*
15. *NAI-1408*
16. *NAI-1341*

17. *NAI-1343*
18. *NAI-1651*
19. *NAI-1389*
20. *NAI-1272*
21. *NAI-1593*
22. C.A. Bayly, 'The pre-History of Communalism? Religious Conflicts in India, 1700-1860', *Modern Asian Studies* 19(11),1985 pp. 172-203. In fact in his zeal to absolve the colonial rulers from creating Hindu-Muslim divide in India, he reaches many hilarious conclusions, e.g. "the form of these land wars was often a savage attack by the totality of rural society against the small town headquarters of the Muslim gentry". This has hardly any basis. Moreover, his assumption that the grantees were generally town-based is again open to question. His other conclusions require some consideration. The destruction of the family graveyards was often referred to in most of these petitions. Should we consider such acts as "a straight forward piece of communal savagery"? "But the complaints of this nature were preferred against the Muslim *zamindar* as well, even the destruction of the books of theology and religion is mentioned in these *mahzars*. Whether these occurrences were the order of the day cutting across religious lines or such things were mentioned only to attract the imperial attention or both is difficult to say.
23. For further details see Zahiruddin Malik, 'Problems of *faujdari* jurisdiction in Baiswara' Aligarh Paper for I.H.C., 1973, pp. 211-15.

Document No. 7. Fascimile of the *mahzar* submitted by the Qazi Maudud from Baiswara region in AD1662, describing the atrocities of the Bais zamindars against his family.

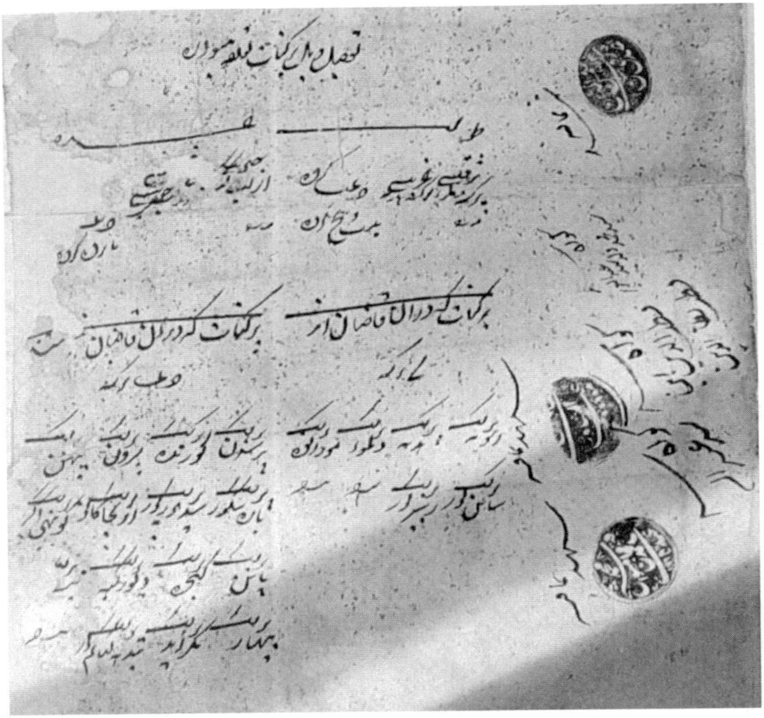

9

Two Madad-i Ma'āsh Farmans of Aurangzeb from Awadh

There exist two early copies of *farmans* issued under the seal of Emperor Aurangzeb conferring *madad-i ma'āsh* grants upon a religious divine of *pargana* Salon and his son. The earlier one was issued to Shaikh Pir Muhammad in the 19th R.Y./AH 1086 (A.D. 1676), while the other was issued to his son, Shaikh Muhammad Ashraf in the 22nd R.Y./A.H. 1090 (A.D 1679). I give annotated translations of these *farmans* in Appendices A and B.[1] The second of these *farmans* has certain uncommon features, which demand some attention. The documents also help us to understand the procedure followed in issuing such grants by the Mughal administration.

The first *farman* (translation in Appendix A) which was issued to Shaikh Pir Muhammad in A.H. 1086 (A.D. 1676) conforms to the routine text of such *farmans*. It has more or less followed the general form, which was set-out by the Mughal chancellery for making such grants. However, there are two points which appear significant. First, this grant was not situated in an *a'imma* village (in the Mughal period grants were often concentrated in villages so styled),[2] but in *jagir* territory. The previous *hukkam* (officers, presumably *jagirdars)* of the village Mirza Bakhtiyarpur had already offered 200 *bighas* of land to the grantee and the imperial *farman* was issued really to confirm the grants, so that the grantee might not be harassed by any future *jagirdar* or any of his officials.[3] Secondly, the words, "an offering to the servants of one knowing mystic truths" *(nazr-i khadiman-haqaiq-o-m'ārif agah)* in the main body of the *farman* as well in *zimn,* show that the grantee was regarded as a mystic enjoying high reputation and hence, considered deserving of the grant.[4]

The second *farman* issued to Shaikh Muhammad Ashraf in the 22nd R.Y. (A.D. 1679), is very important in many ways. First of all, unlike the usual *farman* conferring *madad-i-ma 'ash* grants, it states the *jama* (estimated revenue) and not the area of the grant; it confers the entire village in grant.[5] The *zimn* furthermore gives the *hasil* (revenue realisation) figure from the 4th to the 17th regnal year. This too is unusual.[6] The *zimn* to the *farman* also contains the statement that the grantee had previously settled in the village with the consent *(ba-razamandi)* of the *zamindars.*[7] This seems to imply that the *zamindars* had been unable to meet the revenue demand and therefore transferred their rights to Shaikh Muhammad Ashraf, who now sought tax-exemption from the authorities by way of *madad-i ma'ash.* The village had been nearly abandoned, and its revenue-paying capacity greatly reduced, as figures which appear on the *zimn* on the *farman* show.

A—The total *jama* (estimated-revenue) of the village Singhwal in entirety was 32100 *dams* (= ₹ 802.5)

B—Actual realisation *(hasil)*

Year	*Hasil in ₹*
4th year	50.00
5th year	31.00
6th to 9th years	91.00
10th year	21.00
11th year	26.00
12th year to 16th years	66.00
17th year	61.00

The fact that here the grantee was also now the *zamindar* of the area, might explain yet another feature of the grant, viz., its assignment to the grantee in absolute perpetuity, "generation after generation, and for all time to come."[9] This is interesting since it was only in 34th RY/A.D. 1690 that Emperor Aurangzeb made the *madad-i ma 'ash* hereditary by issuing a general *farman,*[10] whereas our *farman* was issued much before this measure, in A.D. 1679.

The beneficiaries of these grants were the founders of a family of mystics established at Salon (District Rae Bareli, Uttar Pradesh). The tomb of Shaikh Pir Muhammad still exists at Salon. The village Mirzapur Bakhtiyarpur in which he was given 200 *bighas* in AD 1676 can be traced in Nasirabad, the headquarters of the *pargana* in which it lay, is about 14 miles from Salon. The inscription at the main gate of the tomb gives the date of his death as AH. 1099/AD. 1687[11] Shaikh Pir Muhammad must have thus, been alive when his son Shaikh Muhammad Ashraf received the grant of village Singhwal renamed Ashrafabad: According to the chronogram on the same inscription at the main gate of the tomb, he died in AH 1167/ A.D. 1754[12] and a tradition recorded in H.R. Nevill's *Gazetteer* states that he was ninety years at the time of his death.[13] It follows that he was born in AH 1077/AD. 1666-67. At the time of the grant, Muhammad Ashraf then would have been about 13 years of age. Probably he was named a beneficiary in the grant in lieu of his father, who already held a grant as a mystic. Shaikh Muhammad Ashraf's young age explains why no spiritual title is put before his name, contrasting with the respectful address used for his father.[14]

The village of Singhwal Ashrafabad (now called Ashrafganj Singhwal) is situated about 14 miles from Salon. Till the abolition of *zamindari* the family of Shaikh Muhammad Ashraf continued to enjoy *zamindari* as well as *ma 'aft* rights over it, exercised through a scheme of administration drawn up by Mr. Fremantle, the Settlement Officer in 1896.[15]

Procedure for making a revenue-free grant

The person who made copies of these *farman* seems to have been familiar with the styles in which official endorsements were put on the *farman.* Such endorsements are very difficult to decipher, and we are thus, beholden to the copyist for presenting us with deciphered readings, which enable us to reconstruct the procedure followed in issuing the orders for the revenue free grants. Ibn Hasan has provided us with some details of the procedure to the point that the final draft of such *madad-i m 'āsh farman* was made.[16] However, the text of the *zimn* of our two *farmans* together with the endorsements shed much additional light on the procedure followed by the Mughal court and its secretariat or chancellary.

The *zimn* in the first *farman* shows that the procedure in preparing and issuing the *farman* was as follows: First of all an official (in this case, the governor of Allahabad, Himmat Khan)[17] made his recommendation for the grant. This recommendation was presented in written form *(risala)* by the *sadr,* Rizvi Khan[18] to the Emperor during the time of posting of the *waqia-nawis* Inayatullah,[19] on 5th *Rajab* 18th R.Y./25th Sept. A.D. 1675 when the Emperor signified his approval. In accordance with the *tasdiq* (or confirmed record of proceedings) the *yaddasht of waqi 'a* (memorandum of proceedings) was prepared on 14th *Rajab* 18th R.Y/4th Oct. A.D. 1675.

Thereupon the draft of the memorandum was sent to the *wazir (diwan-i 'aala)* Asad Khan[20] and then to the *sadr* Rizvi Khan and both of them verified it, ordering that it should be entered in the record of court proceedings *(waqi'a).* The *waqia-nawis* then certified that the memorandum was same as the record of the proceedings *(waqi'a).* The paper then again was sent to the *wazir,* who ordered that it be submitted a second time *(arz-i mukarrar)* for the Emperor's approval. This was done on 11th *Ramazam*, 19th RY./(29th Nov. A.D. 1675) as certified by the official in charge of *arz-i mukarrar,* Shaikh Abdul 'Aziz.[21] The memorandum now went to the *wazir* whose deputy Bahramand Khan[22] ordered that the *farman* be duly written.

All this text along with some other details was first written out in *shikasta* hand on the back *(zimn)* of the paper that was to bear the *farman* on the front. The *farman* was then written out by the scribe in formal *nasta 'liq* (with the stylised *tughra* written on top and Imperial seal affixed) on 5th *Shawwal* 19th R.Y./ 23rd Dec., A.D. 1675).

The *farman* was now sent to various offices again for verification and record before being handed over to the grantee. It was copied down at the *diwan-i sadarat* (the *sadr's* secretariat) on 12th *Ziqad* 19th R. Y./128th Jan., A.D. 1676, at the office of *a'imma* (land grants) on 9th *Zilhij* 18th RY./124th Feb., A.D. 1676, both offices entering their endorsements on the *zimn*. The *farman* was sent to the office of *taujih*[23] twice on 7th *Zilhij* and 9th *Zilhij* 19th RY. respectively. An interesting point is that the name of Khan Muhammad is mentioned in seven endorsements as the person presenting the *farman* at the endorsing offices. Was he the *wakil* (agent) of the grantee or an official?[24]

From the second *farman* too, it appears from the *zimn* that the same procedure for preparing and issuing the *farman* was followed. Here in this case first of all the *waqi'a nigar* of *suba* of Allahabad, Mir Muhammad Raza Karvi conveyed to the Imperial court that the grantee has settled with the consent of the *zamindar* in the village Singhwal. The provincial *sadr (sadr-i juzv)* Saiyid 'Abdul' Rahim'[25] also sent his recommendation and the reports were presented in written form by the *sadr* Rizvi Khan, to the Emperor during the time of attendance of *waqi'a nawis* Daulatmand khan on 26th *Ziqad* 22nd R.Y./ 29th Dec. A.D. 1679, when the Emperor gave his approval. In accordance with the *tasdiq* (confirmed by the records of proceedings) the *yaddasht* of *waqia* was prepared on 21st *Rabiul Awwal* 22nd RY./ 21st April A.D. 1680.

Thereupon, the draft memorandum was sent to the *wazir* Asad Khan and then to the *sadr* Rizvi Khan for their verification and it was verified by them and ordered that it should be entered in the record of the court proceedings *(waqi'a).* After being verified by the *waqi'a nawis,* the *wazir* ordered that it should be submitted a second time *(ba arz-i mukarrar)* for the Emperor's approval. This was done on 12th *Rabius Sani* 22nd R.Y./12th May A.D. 1680 as certified by the official incharge of *arz-i mukarrar,* Lutfullah Khan,[26] whereafter it reached the *wazir* Asad Khan, who ordered that the *farman* be duly written.

Here too in the *zimn* all this text along with other details was first written out in *shikasta* hand on the back of the paper, which was to bear the *farman* in *nasta'liq* hand on the front. The *farman* itself was written out by the copyist on 18th *Jamadul Awwal* 22nd R.Y./16th June A.D. 1680.

The *farman* thereafter was sent to various offices for verification. But unfortunately it is not possible to decipher these endorsements as they are much torn. However, the number of these endorsements is the same as in the earlier one. So it may be presumed that it went through the same channels before being handed over to the grantee.

The above-mentioned procedure goes to suggest that every possible precaution was taken before the passing of the order by the Emperor and later, for ensuring that the *farman* issued was in actual conformity with what was recorded so as to guard against fraud at any stage. It was undoubtedly a long procedure and in the case of these particular grants it took about four to six months' time before the *farman* could reach the grantee.

APPENDIX 'A'

In the name of the God, the beneficent, the merciful

(TUGHRA)

Copy of the square seal Abul Muzzaffar Muhi-uddin Muhammad 'Alamgir Padshah Ghazi, A.H. 1083. The names of his ancestors beginning with Timur *sahib-i qiran* in circle.

Whereas it had been submitted to the exalted court, that according to the deeds *(asnād)* issued by the officials *(hukkām)* 200 *bighas* of land from the village Mirza Bakhtiyarpur, *pargana* Nasirabad *sarkar* Manikpur, *suba* Allahabad had been made over by way of offering to the servants of the mystic Shaikh Pir Muhammad, resident of *pargana* Salon, and he is in occupation and control of the land above mentioned and entertains the hope that in this regard an Imperial *farman* may be issued; therefore, the world-subduing order is issued that the aforesaid land at the old site, as per previous practice and upon conditions of (the grantee's) actual occupation and control, be given over to him in *madad-i ma 'āsh* in accordance with the particulars on the back *(zimn)* so that he may, appropriating the revenues thereof for his own needs engage himself in praying for the long life of this ever more prosperous Empire—the present and future officials, revenue *collectors, jagirdars* and *karoris* should leave the land aforesaid in his hands and should never allow any transfer or alterations herein and not harass (the grantee) on account of the land-revenue *(mal),* other taxes *(jihat)* and other cesses such as *qunalgah, peshkash, jaribana, zabitlana, muhsilana mahrana, daroghana, begar, shikar, muqqadami, qanungoi* and *zabti harsala,*[27] or insistence upon cultivation, and all fiscal impositions and government dues whatsoever. They shall not demand a confirmatory order every year and if at some other place he (the grantee) has any thing (i.e. land grants), it should not be taken into account (to reduce the present grant). Written on the 5th *Shawwal*, 19th Regnal year.

Zimn

Copy of (court) proceedings, dated Thursday 14th *Rajab*, 18th R.Y. Corresponding to A.H. 1086 (A.D. 1676-77) corresponding to *Ilahi* month, written upon the note *(risala)* of the honoured Saiyid (titles omitted), the highly elevated *sadr,* Rizvi Khan, during the posting as recorder *(waqi'a nawis),* Inayatullah, to wit; upon the recommendation of the governor (titles omitted), Himmat Khan, it has been conveyed to the exalted court that according to the deeds *(asnad)* issued by the *hukkam* (officials, or *jagirdars),* 200 *bighas* of land from the village Mirza Bakhtyarpur, *pargana* Nasirabad, *sarkar* Manikpur, *suba* Allahabad, has been made over as offering to the mystic Shaikh Pir Muhammad, resident of *pargana* of Salon, and he entertains the hope that in this regard an Imperial *farman* may be issued; therefore, the world-subduing order was issued that we confer the aforesaid land at the old site as per previous practice and upon the condition of (the grantee's) occupation and control thereof for their *madad-i maa'sh* and if at some other place he (the grantee) has anything (i.e. land-grants), it should not be taken into account. *Waqia* dated 5th *Rajab* 18th R.Y. Transcribed according to the verification of the memorandum.

Copy of the endorsement of the great minister (titles omitted) Asad Khan; "Enter in record of proceedings."

Copy of endorsement by the Saiyid (titles omitted), the elevated *sadr* Rizvi Khan: Enter in record of proceedings. Copy of endorsement by the *Waqi'a Nawis* : "True copy of proceedings".

Copy of endorsement of the great minister (titles omitted) (Asad Khan): "Let it be submitted for the second presentation".

Copy of the note of the scholarly (titles omitted) Shaikh 'Abdul Aziz: "submitted for second presentation 11th *Ramzan*, 19th R.Y."

Copy of endorsement of (titles omitted) Bahramand Khan acting as deputy of the commander *Jumdat-ul Mulk (Mir*

Bakhshi): "Let the Imperial *farman* be prepared."

"200 bighas of land at the old site be conferred as per previous practice."

Endorsements

1. The *farman* is written down according to the memorandum of the court proceedings.
2. Written down through the agency of Khan Muhammad.
3. Copied down in the office of *diwan-e sadarat* through the agency of Khan Muhammad, dated 12th *Ziqa'da* 19th R.Y.
4. Verified the court proceedings on 14th *Ziqa'da* 19th R.Y. and compared with the entries of the diary dated 14th *Rajab.*
5. Entered in the *awarija.*
6. Copied down in the office of *a'imma* through the agency of Khan Muhammad dated 9th *Zilhij* 19th R.Y./AH. 1086.
7. The copy of the Imperial order was sent to the office of *taujih* for details through the agency of Khan Muhammad on 9th *Zilhij* 19th R.Y.
8. Copy of the Imperial order was sent to the office of the *sahib taujih..........Ziqad* 19th RY./AH. 1086/2nd of the Bahman Ilahi month.
9. Entered in the office of the........ dated 27th *Zilhij* 19th RY./ AH. 1086.

APPENDIX 'B'

In the name of the God, the beneficent, the merciful

(TUGHRA)

> Copy of the square seal Abul Muzzaffar Muhiuddin Muhammad 'Alamgir Padshah *Ghazi* A.H. 1080. Also all the names of his ancestors beginning from Timur *sahib-i qiran* in circle.

Copy of the exalted *farman* demanding obedience, bearing the seal of Abul Muzzaffar Muhiuddin Hazrat 'Alamgir *Padshah Ghazi* addressed to Shah Pir Muhammad Ashraf Saloni.

Whereas, at this time the *exalted farman* has been issued that the village of Singhwal in entirety, in the *pargana* of Salon within *sarkar* of Manikpur, of *suba* Allahabad, which has a *jama* of 32,100 *dams,* should be assigned to Shaikh Muhammad Ashraf, son of Shaikh Pir Muhammad, according to the *zimn,* from the half of *Rabi* harvest, *Qui-il*, so that (the grantee) should spend all revenues for his own use and should busy himself in praying for the welfare of the everlasting Empire, therefore, it is incumbent upon officers, administrators, revenue collectors [present and future] to leave the said village in his possession and recognise it as exempt from all taxes and demands. In this respect every year the renewal orders should not be demanded (from the grantee) and if at some other place he (the grantee) has anything (i.e. land-grant), it should not be paid attention to. Dated 18th *Jamadul Awwal,* 22nd R.Y.

Zimn

Copy of the (court) proceedings *(yaddashi-i waqi'a)* dated Wednesday 21st *Rabi-ul-Awwal*, 22nd R.Y./AH 1090 *Ilahi* month...by the honoured Saiyid (titles omitted), the highly elevated *sadr* Rizvi Khan, during the posting as recorder *(waqi'a nawis)* of Daulatmand, to wit; and according to the letter of Mir Muhammad Raza Karvi, the *waqi'a nigar* of the province of Awadh, it has been conveyed to the exalted court that Shaikh Muhammad Ashraf, son of the mystic Shaikh Pir Muhammad, resident of *pargana* Salon, *sarkar* Manikpur, *suba* Allahabad, who is adorned with perfection, has settled with the consent of the *zamindars,* in the village Singhwal under the aforesaid *pargana* and has renamed it Ashrafabad. Saiyid 'Abdur Rahim, the provincial *sadr (sadr-i juzv)* of Allahabad, has also sent his recommendation. And Shaikh Muhammad Ashraf entertains the hope that world-subduing order be issued that the aforesaid village has been conferred in its entirety as his *madad-i ma'ash* for generations to come. And if at some other place he (the grantee) has anything (i.e. land-grants), it should not be taken into account *waqia.* Dated 26th *Ziqad,* 22nd R.Y. Transcribed according to the Register of proceedings *(fard-i yaddasht).* Copy of endorsement of the great minister (titles omitted) Asad Khan, "Enter in the record of (court) proceedings *(yaddasht).*"

Copy of endorsement by the honoured Saiyid (titles omitted) highly elevated *sadr* Rizvi Khan, "Enter in the *waqi'a.*" Copy of endorsement by the *waqi'a-nawis* "Is in accordance with the *waqi'a*" : Copy of the endorsement by (titles) Asad Khan: "Let this be put up for second presentation *(arz-i mukarrar)",* Copy of endorsement of (titles) Lutfullah Khan, "On the 12th *Rabi-ul Awwal* 22 R.Y., submitted for the second time *(ba-arz-i mukarrar)* to the Emperor." Copy of endorsement of (titles) Asad Khan: "Let the Imperial *farman* be prepared".

(*Hasil* figures of the said village)

Year	*In ₹*
4th year	50.00
5th year	31.00
6th to 9th year	91.00
10th year	21.00
11th year	26.00
12th to 16th year	66.00
17th year	61.00

References

1. I was introduced to these *farmans* by my late father Hazrat Saiyid Shah Muhammad Husain Jafri, the IXth *Sajjada Nashin* (1966-79) of the *Khanqah* of Salon. I had many useful discussions with him about the family history and other related matters. The documents are still preserved in my family collection. [see pp. 182-3 and pp. 184-5 for the dicphered text of both the farmans.
2. Akbar in the year AD 1578, had issued an order by which he had concentrated all the existing grants in certain village, and ordered that all the new grants should also be made from the lands of these villages. It was a precautionary measure, to prevent the grantee from unlawfully acquiring grants in two places. Cf. Irfan Habib, *Agrarian System of Mughal India,* p. 301.
3. Since a *jagirdar* could assign a grant only for his term of assignment, which was a few years duration, the new *jagirdar* might or might not respect the order of his predecessor. So this class of grantees lived in the greatest insecurity. They were, therefore, always anxious to obtain the confirmation of such assignment from the Court to escape eviction by future *jagirdar. Ibid.,* pp. 315-16.
4. See the text as well as the *zimn* in plate no. I.
5. All the *madad-i ma'ash* grants were as a rule, made in terms of definite area stated in *bighas.* But there are some exceptions most of them from the earlier period. Two of Babur's *farmans* simply name the village and in one of them its *jama 'raqmi* is also stated. Akbar's *farman* of 1567 relating to Jalandhar, names the village and specifies its *jama'* but not the area. Aurangzeb's *farman* of 35th R.Y. relating to Pattan (Gujarat) omits area but gives both *jama'* and *hasil* of the village. (Irfan Habib, *op. cit.,* p. 30I). A *farman* coming from a later period, of Shah 'Alam II issued in 21st RY/AD 1779. relating to Pachcha, Tirhut omits the area and gives the total *jama.* K.K. Dutta, *Some Farmans' Sanads and Parwanas,* Patna, 1962, p. 10.

6. Irfan Habib, *Agrarian System.* p. 301.
7. See the *zimn* of the second *farman* (Appendix B).
8. The grantees did not by virtue of their grant possess proprietary rights. They were obliged to pay the *huquq-i milkiyat* to the *zamindars.* (Irfan Habib, *op. cit.,*) pp. 300-1.
9. See the *zimn* : Appendix B.
10. Irfan Habib, *op. cit.,* pp. 306-7.
11. The tomb is commonly known as the *Rauza-i Ashrafi;* the chronograms on inscriptions of the main gate of the tomb are still to be seen. These have been published in Thomas Beale, *Miftah ut-Tawarikh,* Nawal Kishore, Kanpur, 1867, pp. 286, 335.
12. See the preceeding footnote.
13. H.R. Nevill, *District Gazetteers of United Provinces of Agra and Oudh* (Rae Bareli) Vol. XXXIX, Lucknow, 1923, pp. 100-3.
14. See the *zimn* and the main text in the two Appendices.
15. H.R. Nevill, *op. cit.,* Vol. XXXIX, pp. 102-3. After the abolition of the *zamindari* in 1952, an annuity was made of these *zamindari* and *ma'āfi* villages and now the expenditure is made by the present *Sajjada Nashin* Saiyid Shah Ahmad Husain Jafri Islahi in accordance with the scheme of administration drawn up by the Civil Judge, Rae Bareli (U.P.). (Regular Suit No. I of 1950 decided on 31-7-1953, Sunni Central Board of Waqfs, Lucknow vs. Shah Muhammad Naim Ata Sajjada Nashin).
16. Ibn Hasan, *Central Structure of the Mughal Empire.* Delhi, 1970, pp. 92-106.
17. The governor of *suba* Allahabad from 18th R.Y. to 24th R.Y (1675-81 A.D.)—Cf. M. Athar Ali, 'Provincial Governors under Aurangzeb,' *Medieval India—A Miscellany,* Vol. I, p. 108.
18. He was the *sadr-us sudur* of Aurangzeb during 10th R.Y. to 24th R.Y. and also held *mansab* of 3000 *zat* 500 *sawars. Ma 'asir-ul Umara,* Vol. II, p. 558; see also in M. Athar Ali, *Mughal Nobility under Aurangzeb,* pp. 87, 237.
19. This officer might be the same as the famous Inayatullah Khan Kashmiri, who later rose to prominence and in 49th R.Y. got the *mansab* of 2500 *zat/250 sawar* Cf. Shah Nawaz Khan, *Ma 'asir-ul Umara* tr. H Beveridge, Kolkata, 1941, Vol. I, pp 680-82.
20. The well-known *wazir* of Aurangzeb held the *mansab* of 7000 *zat/ 7000 sawars. Cf Ibid.,* Vol. I, p. 271.
21. He held the *mansab* of 1500 *zat/500 sawar* during this period. cf. *Ibid.* Vol. I, p. 34.

22. He held the rank of 7000 *zat/7000 sawars,* and was always assigned the financial and executive duties. cf. Athar Ali, *op. cit.,* pp. 145, 217.
23. Where the office records of pay-assignments, etc. were kept, See Khwaja Yasin's *Glossary*, Patna, private collection (Rotograph in the Department of History, AMU, Aligarh No. 244).
24. See the *zimn* in the Appendix A.
25. No information on this official record has been found.
26. He held the rank of 1500 *zat/500 sawars.* In 2nd RY he was made the officer-in-charge of *arz-i mukkarrar,* M.U., Vol. I, p. 838.
27. All these taxes and perquisites have been explained in B.N. Goswami and J.S. Grewal, *The Mughals and the Jogis of Jakhbar,* Simla, 1967, and so do not require elucidation here.

10

Landed Properties of a Sufi Establishment-Calendar of 17th 19th Century Documents from Salon in Awadh

The various original documents as well as the letters of Mughal and Nawabi periods; preserved in the private collections of the family members of the mystic establishment at Salon (situated in Rae Bareli district) relate to *madad-e ma'ash* grant held by Shaikh Pir Muhammad and his family from the 17th Century to recent times.[1] Since here we have an authentic account of the land-rights of a mystic family, setting its roots in the soil from below, the documents and the history they expose, are of great interest. They also shed light on administrative policies from time to time. Here and there, however, our subject is also illuminated by the narrative sources and recorded traditions.

A Calender of the documents has been prepared at the end, and each document is assigned a number for easy reference. Full text as well as the extracts of some important documents has been appended at the end of the paper.

(i) **Procedure of the *madad-e-ma'ash* grant:** The family of the mystic established at Salon claim to the Faruqi

Shaikhs, and say that while their original home was Yeman, they had settled in Nagor, the celebrated Qazi Hamid Uddin of Nagor (d. 1244) belonging to his branch. The family is said to have migrated from Nagor to Jaunpur during the period of the Sharqi Sultans. Makhdum Shaikh Addhan (d. 1568) became famous as a *sufi* saint, and from him the family members acquired the name of *Addhani*. One of his descendants, Shaikh Abdul Nabi settled at Salon and here in 996 AH/1578 Shaikh Pir Muhammad was born. After early education, he went to Manikpur for higher studies in rational and religious sciences. He became a disciple of Shaikh Abdul Karim (d. 1647), the sajjada - nasheen of the khanqah of Shaikh Husam ul Haque Manikpur (d. 1470). After remaining there for quite some time under his spritual guidance and according to his instructions, Shaikh Pir Muhammad returned to Salon and according to a later tradition took up his abode here along with a *sanyasi* hermit.

It appears that Shaikh Pir Muhammad soon acquired prominance sufficient to merit the attention of the local officials. As they made over to him, 'by way of an offering for the servant of one knowing mystic truths' a grant of 200 *bigha* land in village Mirzapur Bakhtiyar, *pargana* Nasirabad, *sarkar* Manikpur *suba* Allahabad. Since presumably the grant was initially made by one of the *hukkam* or *jagirdars*, and so temporary in nature (co-terminal with the *jagir*-assignment), so an imperial *farman* was issued on 5th, *shawwal* 19th RY 1676 recognizing the *madad-e-maash* rights of the grantee on these 200 *bighas* and requiring that the grantee be not harrassed by the future officials (Doc. No. 1).

Shaikh Pir Muhammad's son, Shaikh Muhammad Ashraf was assigned the revenue of a village Singhwal, *pargana* Nasirabad, *sarkar* Manikpur *suba* Allahabad, by the *zamindars* of the village. A perusal of the *hasil* figures of the village from 4th RY to 17th RY suggest that the revenue paying capacity of the village was greatly reduced; hence the *zamindars* were unable to meet the revenue demand and so transferred their rights to Shaikh Muhammad Ashraf who now sought tax exemption from the authorities, soliciting a *madad-e-ma'ash* grant. The assignment to the grantee was ultimately made in absolute perpetuity on 18th *jamad* I 22nd RY/ AD 1679. (Doc. No. 2).

Emperor Aurangzeb, before proceeding to the Deccan is said to have invited Shaikh Pir Muhammad to pay a visit to Delhi (Doc. No. 3); but the offer was politely refused. (Doc. No. 4).

Subsequent to the above grants (Doc. Nos. 1 &2) Aurangzeb is said to have assigned the revenues of the village Palhipur to Shaikh Muhammad Ashraf in AH 1109/AD 1697 as the *Waqia-nawis* of the area informed the court that the present income of the mystic was not sufficient to meet his expenses. Probably, with the similar consideration and procedure. Emperor Bahadur Shah assigned the revenues of village Kishandaspur to Shaikh Muhammad Ashraf in 1119/ AD 1707.[2]

It appears that Shaikh Muhammad Ashraf came to possess a number of residential plots and superior land rights in a number of *chaks* (land strips) and villages in *sarkar* Manikpur, *suba* Allahabad as well as in *sarkar* Lucknow, *suba* Akhtarnagar Awadh either through imperial favour or through local officials and even by the *zamindars*. All these acquisitions were now confirmed by Emperor Muhammad Shah on 19th *Rabi* II/10th RY/AD 1729 through an imperial *farman* (Doc. No. 5).

The next imperial *farman* was issued by Emperor Shah Alam II who is said to have held Shah Muhammad Panah (d. 1785) in high esteem. The latter requested the Emperor for a comprehensive *farman* in line of all other *farmans* and *parwanahs* he had received from time to time. He send all the copies of such orders along with a list of his possessions which included a large number of villages, *chaks*, gardens and residential quarters (*havelies*) situated in *suba* Allahabad and Awadh. It was also solicited that the new *farman* be issued in the name of his son Shah Karim Ata (d. 1833). Accordingly, when Emperor held his *darbar* at Allahabad, the said *farman* was issued on 15th Safar 6th RY/AD 1778 (Doc. No. 6).

The exact details of the manner in which favours were bestowed upon these mystics by local chiefs and *zamindars* are unfortunately missing. Still some idea can be formed by the perusal of some statements included in 19th century colonial records, known as *wajib-ul 'arz* (spelt 'wajib-ool urz') compiled during the course of first regular settlement of the province of Oudh after events of 1857. These papers recorded the 'past history of the village from the earliest period to which it can be conventiently traced: on the basis of this village-wise information the history of the families and clans was arranged and finally incorporated in the settlement reports.

A few *wajib-ul'arz* statements of the villages which were included in the revenue grants of these mystics are available. A perusal of the first paragraphs of these statements (which deal with the history of village concerned) give some idea of the procedure adopted in these grants. The following may serve for examples.

1. Village Dhankesra, *pargana* Parshadepur and village Barwaliya, *pargana* Salon belonged to Raja Balbhadra Singh, the Kanhpuria chieftain of Tilain. He donated the revenue of these two villages for feeding the poor, mandicants, and visitors to the *khanqah* of Shah Muhammad Panah. These grants were confirmed by the imperial *farman* (Doc. No. 6).

2. The Rajas of *ta'alluqa* Bhadri, *pargana* Behar had allotted two tracts of forest land to Shah Muhammad Panah. The grantee was to get the forest cleared and the area settled with peasant castes especially the kurmis. One tract was named Panah Nagar, and another Hayat Nagar (after the name of his deceased brother Muhammad Hayat).

3. A tract of forest land was also granted by Emperor Shah Alam II to Shah Karim 'Ata. The grantee got the land cleared from forest, settled the population (mostly kurmis) and named it after his father as Panah Nagar.

The existance of a large number of the villages having the nomenclature similar to that of the family members of the mystic establishment lead us to conclude that large tracts of waste land might have been cleared by these grantees to settle the population and, in turn, raise their income.

Donald Buttler gives a detailed account of this establishment in 1836. He says that the original proprietors of the town of Salon were Kanhpuria Rajputs who were deprived of their estate in Salon *khas* by Nawab Asafuddoulah (d. 1797), it was then bestowed upon the mystic family for perpetual support of the religious "eleemasynary" establishment.

The establishment seems to have been the largest of its kind in the southern parts of Awadh. The annual income was estimated by Donald Buttler (1836) at ₹ 30,000/- all of which was utilized in entertaining *bairagis* and *faqirs* with out making any distinction of religion. The visitors used to flock to the *khanqah* in quite large numbers and at time there might happpen to be about 100 mendicants. These were attended to and looked after by the *sajjada-nashin* of the *khanqah*. The head of the institution (*sajjada-nashin*) was held in high esteem by the local officials. His reputation was such that whenever the *chakledar* came to Salon, he always paid a visit to the mystic and offered him a few hundred rupees as nazr.[3]

The inmates of the establishment, it seems, did not have any sympathy for the religious zeal of the *wahabis* under Saiyid Ahmad of Rae Bareli (d. 1831). He was told by the *zamindar* of the area and the *sajjada nashin* that they considered aiding the poor and blind as more pious than indulging in holy war. Similarly, they refused to abandon the ceremonies associated with the rituals in the month of *muharram*[4]

W.H. Sleeman, while undertaking the tour in the kingdom of Oudh (1849-50) refers to this establishment as the prime mystic institution of the kingdom. Shah Panah 'Ata (d. 1860), the then *sajjada-nashin* of the *khanaah* was looked upon with great reverence by both Muslims and Hindus for the sanctity of his ancestors and the institution. He did not go out of the *Khanqah* but remained there to received the homage and distribute food to the needy travellers of all religions. Sleeman estimated the annual income from the grant held by him in AD 1850 at about ₹ 25,000.

In addition to the income from revenue free grants assigned by the Awadh rulers, the local officials as well as the princes in the distant places such as Bhopal and Sironj made substantial offerings. This way the actual income of the establishment was calculated to amount to about ₹ 50,000 a year. Complimentary letters were sent to 'Shah Punah 'Ata' by the Governor General of India, and Lieutenant Governors of the NW Provinces. When Sleemen was passing through the district of Salon 'Shah Punah Ata sent him "letter of compliments and welcome with a present of a tame antelope, and some fruits and sugar". This good will gesture was reciprocated by Sleeman, who got the impression that "his character is held in high esteem by all classes of the people, of whatever creed, caste or grade.[5]

After the annexation of Awadh an enquiry was instituted to examine the credentials of these grantees. Major Barrow was appointed to conduct it; the then grantee Shah Husain 'Ata deposited 31 *farmans, sanads* and *parwanas* with the authorities on 15th June 1856 and obtained a receipt for them. But all these documents were destroyed during the Mutiny. The second enquiry could start only after the events of 1857. The details of the enquiry conducted by WC Wood, now forms a historical narrative giving the family history, details of the income and expenditure and the status of these grants. On the basis of this enquiry Lord Canning issued a *sanad* to Shah Husain 'Ata on 26.9.1862, recognising his all allodial rights over the 22 villages of his grant. The *sanad* was issued subjected to the condition that the grant was to continue so long as the income is devoted to the maintenances of the *Khanqah* buildings, tombs, masques, running of a school of 'Muhammadan Education' and the continuation of the charities as detailed in the sanad.[7]

(ii) **Law of succession and family custom:** The succession to the office of the *sajjada-nashin* was determined by a complex system of custom and coventions. Inheritance in matter of landed properties attached to the office took a definite form after undergoing a number of experiments. There appears to have been no problem till Shah Karim 'Ata succeed his father Shah Muhammad Panah, as before this time all the prospective claimants had predeceased their fathers. Since Shah Karim 'Ata had five sons (two of whom died in infancy) hence, there arose the necessity to set out certain norms for future succession. At an earlier stage he himself had divided all his possessions including buildings, villages, *chaks*, gardens, books and even relies, equally among his three sons, reserving one village for his daughter.[8] But partly due to the fact the Awadh Court was not melined to approve such a scheme for division, and also since his eldest son Shah Ashraf 'Ata (d. 1824) had expired after sometimes, the earlier arrangement had to be annulled and a new *Iqrarnamah* was executed by Shah Karim Ata in favour of his second son Shah Panah 'Ata on 6th Jamad I 1244 AH/1827 AD. This paper is of importance for spelling out the *waqf* characrter of the properties attached with the institution and the position of the other members of the family in relation to the *sajjadanashin*. In fact an institution was sought to be established as the new arrangement entailed that all the books, relies and the building of the *Khanqah*, tombs, mosques and the madrasa were to be maintained and looked-after by the incumbents to the office of *sajjada nashin*.[9] The successor to this office could theoretically be chosen from amongst the sons, relatives, devotees and even from amongst strangers. The news of such nomination was to be always communicated to the Mughal emperor (Doc. No. 6) This practice seems to have continued during the days of the *nawab wazirs* also. The approval was sought from the government for appointing a successor *sajjada nashin* and *mutawalli* (custodian). It seems that by the first half of the 19th century the office of the *mutawalli* came to be possessed by the spiritual head of the institution (*sajjada nashin*) himself. Our documents do not provide any clueas to when the existing deference between these two offices was done away with. Both offices were made hereditary and permanent. (Doc. No. 7)

The customs and the conventions peculiar to the family of the mystics were recognised by the British authorities during the first regular settlement of the province of Awadh after the annexation. These were made part of and incorporated in the *Rawaj-e-aam* document of the *parganas* where the *maafi* villages of the grantee were situated. In the preamble of the *Rawaj-e-aam*, *pargana* Parshadepur *tehsil* Salon, it is explicity admitted by the *ta'alluqadars, numberdars* and the *maafidars*, that the "legal settlement of the villages belonging to us had been made for a period of thirty years and hence, all the privileges particulars to us had been described in detail, while the general rules applicable in the region had been omitted. We agree to abide by these. "The superior land-right holders were asked to state their family custom, with regard to six sections, subdivided into twenty two questions. The main features of the family of *Sajjada nashin* were as under:

(a) The lawful heir and the legal representative of the *sajjada nashin* could only be a *sajjada nashin*. The latter was to be nominated by the previous incumbent in his life-time by observing certain customary ceremonies and rituals in a prescribed manner as detailed in the document itself.

(b) All other heirs of the *sajjada nashin* including his widow, were not entitled to any share in the landed or urban properties left by the deceased. These heirs could *claim* only a subsistance allowance known as *quzara*. The widow and unmarried daughters of the deceased were to be looked after by the future incumbent to the office of the *sajjada nashin*.

(c) The *sajjada nashin* was only a custodian of the properties either held as *waqf* or *maafi* and thus, he was not empowered to affect any change by way of sale or mortgage or by oral gift.

(iii) **Nawab wazirs policy towards *aimma* holders:** Ghulam Ali Azad Bilgirami (d. 1761) criticizes Burhanul Mulk Saadat Ali Khan and Safdarjung for resuming cash and land grants (*wazaif-o-suyurghalat*) of the old and the new families. As a result of this he says that Muslim learning suffered very heavily in both Awadh and Allahabad provinces. He does not himself attribute this explicitly to any sectarian motive on the part of the two Awadh rulers; and it is possible to argue that the motives were purely financial. The members of scholarly families, says Azad Bilgirmi had to take to the military profession

> as a result of these measures, a curious statement which suggests that a connection was always maintained between the grant-holders and the army.[9]

Elsewhere it has been argued that as a result of the laxity in the administrative machinary during the first half of the 18th century quite a few grants were obtained by the fraudulent means and perhaps, the *nawab-wazirs* tried to weed out such grants and to confirm only the genuine ones.[10]

But a perusal of the 18th century documents of the family in the private collection of Shah Muhammed Hameed 'Ata Hassan (now residing at Karachi, Pakistan) suggest that an open policy of resumption of the *aimma* grant was pursued by the first three *nawabs*, and it was a matter of rare favour if some of the *aimma* grants escaped confiscation or the grantees were given back their grants after the resumption.

A letter addressed by Shah Muhammad Panah to Burhanul Mulk Saadat Khan clearly mentions that in compliance of his orders regarding the resumption of the *aimma* (*bar-zabti-e-aimma-e-subajat*) grants the troops have been posted by the '*amils* in every hook and corner including the villages of grantee. Although the grantee was in possession of a *parwana* for all the villages, still the *gumasthas* (agents) of Murshid Quli Khan were demanding a fresh *parwana* addressed to them. (Doc. No. 8).

The fact at the policy of resumption was persued by Safdarjung in full vigour is borne out by two of his *parwanas* issued to the local officials regarding the affairs of the villages included in the grant of these mystis. In *parwana* addressed to Raja Ram Narain, the *wazir* in the first RY it was conveyed that the revenues of village Barwaiya in entirety along with the *Chaks* is granted to meet the expenses of the medicants residing at the *khanqah* of Shaikh Muhammad Ashraf (d. 1754). It should be recognised by the *amils* of the area and no interference be allowed with (Doc. No. 9). The other *parwana* was issued in the 6th RY to Zainul 'Abidin Khan stipulating that the village Barwaliya, was earlier resumed and included in the *khalisa*, has been restricted to the possession of Shaikh Muhammad Ashraf and Shah Pir 'Ata. Now the descendants of the former *aimmadars* who held the land previously were interfereing with the above mentioned village and *chaks* attached thereto, which is illegal. they should be asked to keep off the village and it should be recognised as the *aimma* (land) of the lawful grantees. Confirmatory orders should not be demanded from them every year (Doc. No. 10).

The resumption of revenue grants continued during Shujaud Daulah's (d. 1775) period also. In a letter addressed to Shah Muhammad Panah the *nawab* specifically says that no orders have been issued to any '*amils* for the resumption of the *aimma* land of the addressee. If advertantly any interference has been committed, a *shuqqa* is being sent by hand which will further eliminate any such possibility (Doc. No. 11).

An acute financial crisis seems to have been responsible for *nawab-wazirs* to bring all the land under *khalisa* and put it under their direct administration. We know for certain that almost all the Mugal *jagirdars* had leased out their *jagirs* to Burhanul Mulk on *ijara* tenures as they themselves found it quite difficult to collect the land revenue from their assignments.[11] Similarly, Safdarjung had reportedly instructed his *wakil* at the Mughal Court to invite the imperial attention towards the heavy expenditure incurred by the *nawab* in the administration of the two provinces, and hence, no new *jagirs* were to be assigned in these provinces.[12]

Appendix A: Sajjda-Nashins of *Khanqah* at Salon

1. Shaikh Pir Muhammad (died 1687 AD) nominated by Shaikh Abdul Karim (d. 1647) of Manikpur

2. Shaikh Pir Muhammad Ashraf (died 1754) nominated by 1
3. Shah Pir Muhammad Panah (died 1785) nominated by 2
4. Shah Muhammad Karim 'Ata (died 1833) nominated by 3
5. Shah Muhammad Panah 'Ata (died 1860) nominated by 4
6. Shah Muhammad Husain 'Ata (died 1880) nominated by 5
7. Shah Muhammad Mehdi 'Ata (died 1900) nominated by 6
8. Shah Muhammad Naeem 'Ata (died 1966) nominated by 7
9. Shah Muhammad Husain Jafri (died 1979) nominated by 8
10. Shah Husain Jafri Islahi, nominated by 9 (the present Sajjada-nashin of the Kanqah)

Appendix B

Document No. 1: Farman of Aurangzeb 5th Shawwal 19th RY/ AD 1675

"Wheras it has been submitted to the exalted court, that according to the deeds (*asnad*) issued by the officials (*hukkam*) 200 *bighas* of land from the village Mirzapur Bhakhtiyar, pargana Nasirabad, *sarkar* Manikpur, *suba* Allahabad has been made over by way of offering to the servants of the one knowing mystic truths (*nazr khạdiman haqaiqo m'aarif agah*) Shaikh Pir Muhammad, and he is in actual possession of the land above mentioned and entertains the hope that in this regard an imperial *farman* may be issued; therefore, the world subduring order is given over to him in *madad-i-ma'ash* in accordance with the particulars on the *zimn*, so that he may, appropriating revenues there of for his own needs and engage himself in praying for the long life of the ever prosperous empire. Either imperial officers or those of the *jagirdars* should not allow any alternation leaving the land in hand's of the grantee, they should not harass the grantee on account of land revenue or other taxes and cesses (details omitted), or by insisting upon cultivation, and all fiscal impositions and government dues whatsoever. Confirmatory orders should not be demanded every year by the grantees and if at some other place the grantee has any thing (land grants), it should not be taken into account (to reduce the present grant). Written on the 5th *Shawwal*, 19th Regional Year)."

Doc. No. 2: Farman of Aurangzeb 18th Jamad I 22nd RY 1679 AD.

"Whereas, at this time the exalted *farman* has been issued that the village Singhwal in entirely, *pargana* Salon, *sarkar* Manikpur, *suba* Allahabad, having a *jama* of 32,000 dams should be assigned to Shaikh Muhammad Ashraf as *madad-i-ma'ash* according to the *zimn*, from the half of *Rabi Qui II*, so that the assignee should spend all revenues for his own use, and should busy himself in praying for the welfare of the everlasting empire, therefore, it is incumbent upon the present and future officials to leave the said village in the possession of the grantee and should recognise it exempt from all the taxes and demands. Renewal orders should not be demanded by the grantee every year and if at some other place he has anything it should not be paid attention to, dated 18th *Jamad-ul- Awwal* 22nd RY."

Zimn

"Court proceeding dated 21 *Rabi* I 22nd RY by the *Sadr* Rizvi Khan during the posting of Daulatmand Khan *waqai-nawis*; according to the letter of Mir Muhammad Raza Garvi, the *waqai-nigar* of the province of Allahabad, it has been conveyed to the exalted court that Shaikh Muhammad Ashraf has settled with the consent of the *zamindars* in the village Singhwal under the aforesaid *pargana* and has named it Ashrafabad. Saiyid 'Abdul Rahim *sadr-juzv* of Allahabad has also sent his recommendations. He entertains the hope that world subduing order was issued that the aforesaid village has been conferred in its entirely as his *madad-maash* for generations to come.

Hasil figures of the said village:

1.	4th RY	₹ 50
2.	5th RY	₹ 31
3.	6th RY to 9th RY	₹ 91
4.	10th RY	₹ 21
5.	11th RY	₹ 26
6.	12th RY to 16th RY	₹ 66
7.	17th RY	₹ 61

Doc. No. 3 : Letter ascribed to Emperor Aurangzeb, undated

Addressed to (Shaikh Pir Muhammad) with high regards. After salutations - whereas at this time the emperor) is preoccupied with the suppression of the turbulence in Deccan hence, it is not possible for (him) to pay a visit to the Shaikh. If the Shaikh is coming to Delhi to visit the shrines of his pirs, he would welcome meeting him.

Doc. No. 4: Letter ascribed to Shaikh Pir Muhammad in reply to Aurangzeb, undated:

Emperor, the protector of the religion this mendicant finds no courage (to attend the royal summons) as what a rustic has to do at the royal court (*in dahqani raba bazm sultan the kar*)? If perchance some one happens to visit the (Khanqah) he is welcome; and *Karim* dependent upon none. He cares me when I am hungry, if sin is committed by me, He protects me out. His favours are sufficient for me and to strive for more will be a useless ambition.

Doc. No. 5: *Farman* of Emperor Muhammad Shah 19th Rabi II 10th RY 1729

The plots of residential and agricultural land, villages, *chaks*, villages in *sarkar* Manikpur, *suba* Allahabad and villages in *sarkar* Lucknow *suba* Akhtarnagar Awadh have been in conferment upon Shaikh Muhammad Ashraf according to *farman*, deeds of the officials and *zamindars*. This time also, as per previous practice, the grant is confirmed in *madad-e-maash*. It is ordered that the grantee be allowed to appropriate the revenue thereof and engage himself in praying for the empire. It is incumbent upon the present and future *'ammal*; *jagiirdars* and the *karoris* to abide by the imperial orders by allowing the grantees (to appropriate the revenue) from the villages, *dehats* and *chaks* as detailed in the *zimn* generations after generations and for all the times to come. The grantee should not be harassed on accounmt of *maf-o jihat*, *sair-ikhrajat* (details omittted) *sanads* of confirmation should not be demanded from the grantee every year and if at some other place the grantee has anything it should not be taken into account. *Rabi* II 10th RY.

Doc. No. 6: *Farman* of Shah 'Alam II 15th *Safar* 6th RY

Various villages *chaks*, gardens, and residential apartments in *suba* Allahabad and Akhtarnagar Awadh have been conferred upon Pir Muhammad Ashraf of Salon according to the *farmans*, and deeds of officials and *zamindars*; From the beginning of *kharif yichi II*, all of the above are confirmed as *madad-e-maash* to Shar Pir Karim 'Ata, so that he may appropriate the revenue thereof for his own needs and engage himself in praying for the continuity of the empire. It is incumbent upon the officials, revenue collectors, *mutassadis*, *jagirdars* present and future *karoris* to abide by the orders of the sublime court. They should see to it that all these properties are held by the grantees generation after generation and for all the times to come. the grantee should not be harassed on account of *mal-o-jihat*, *sair-we-ikhrajat* (details omitted) Dated 15th *safar* 6th RY.

Zimn

Details of the *yaddasht waqia*. List of the *dehats*, *chaks*, gardens and residential *havelis suba* Allahabad, *sarkar* Manikpur.

Villages	-	44
Chaks	-	21
Arazi	-	114 *bighas* 8 *biswa*

(i) *Pargana* Salon: Haweli with Painbagh, Karimgunj with old fort, Pirnagar Mohiuddinpur, Muhammadabad, Palhipur, 'Atagunj Usari, Khwajpur, 'Atanagar, Takiya Bahadur, Gulabibagh, Ashrafnagar Bin ghwal, Barwaliya Ramipur, Musafirkhana (7 bighas) Madhopur Ninaiyan.

(ii) *Pargana* Jais: Kesarya, Mahoba

(iii) *Pargana* Nasirabad: Dhankisra, Pirangunj, Mirzapur

(iv) *Pargana* Dalmau: Amrudpur

(v) *Pargana* Kara: Afzalpur Saton (*Zamindari* of the grantee), Mirzapur, Pura Muhammad Saeed

(vi) *Pargana* Manikpur - Bihar

(vii) *Pargana* Rai Bareli - U.P.

Chaks - Ashrafgunj, Panahnagar Dharai, Karimnagar Rewli, *chak* Atarthariya, 'Atanagar Baron (in *pargana* Dhingwas).

Suba Akhtarnagar Awadh, *sarkar* Lucknow 4 *parganas* (i) *pargana* Bijnor - village Ashrafnagar, (ii) Amethi, village Bheta (iii) Rasoli, Karimnagar Sirsaon.

Doc. No. 7: *Farman* of Nasiruddin Haidar, 27th Rajab 1251

Addressed to Maulvi Shah Muhammad Panah 'Ata Be it known to the present and future *mutassadis*, *pargana* Salon that Shah Karim 'Ata had three sons, of whom he nominated Shah Panah 'Ata as sajjada-nashin and *mutawalli* of all the landed possessions. Approval of the sublime court was sought (for these acts) which was granted. The villages, *chaks* gardens, and buildings situated at the *parganas* of Salon, Parshadpur, Jais, Manikpur, and Bihar held by the grantees as *madad-e-maash* from olden times, for meeting out the expenses of *Aeras-e aimma-e-athār,* Khanqahs, and Mosques, are now confirmed in the name of Shah Panah 'Ata and thereafter his sajjada Nashin Shah Husain 'Ata in perptuity and for all times to come. It is incumbent upon the present and future *nazims*, *jagirdars*, *mutassadis* of the said *parganas* to abide by this order. The grantee should not be harassed on account of the taxes like *bhent*, *begar*, *jaribana* and *nazrana*. Neither should he be asked for the dues on account of *faujdar*i, *tehsildari*, and pattadari, confirmatory *sanads* should not be demanded from him every year.

Doc. No. 8: Letter of Shaikh Muhammad Ashraf to Burhanul Mulk, undated

After due regards and salutations expresses his happiness and satisfaction over the extermination of Fakharjung, the rebel congratulations to the *nawab* that by the grace of Almighty God he is able to establish the tenants of Islam in this region. Invites his attention to his orders for the resumption of *aimma* (grants) of the *subas* (Awadh and Allahabad); consequently every where the *sawars* and *piyadas* have been posted by the '*amils* of the nawab including in the villages of the grantee (the petitioner). Says that despite the fact that he has the *parwana* of nawab for all his villages, the *gumashtas* of Murshhid Quli Khan are demanding a *parwana*, addressed specifically to them. Solicits the issue of a *parwana* (to the *gumashtas*) of Murshid Quali Khan to the effect that no interference be committed in the village of Muhammad Ashraf. If this is not done, the maintenance of the Khanqah and the mendiicants will become difficult.

The endorsement of the *nawab* at the right-hand margin on the top of the letter is as under:

Whereas due to the grace of the innocent Imams, the Muslim saints and companions, the extermination of the rebel was possible, it will strengthen the cause of Islam. With regard to the villages you have submitted, a *parwana* (to the *gumashta*) by name is being sent.

Doc. No. 9: *Parwana* of Safdarjung, 15th *Ramzan* Ist RY/ 1167 AH

Addressed to Raja Ram Narain, the Wazib village Barweliya in entirely with the *chaks*, *pargana* Salon who granted for the expenses of the mendicants of Shaikh Muhammad Ashraf. Zainul 'Abidin Khan solicited a *parwana* in his name and stood as surity. Therefore, it is ordered that the '*amils* of that place should consider the said village in the grant of Shaikh Muhammad Ashraf and should not interfere with them so that they may engage themselves in praying for the welfare of the principality.

Doc. No. 10: *Parwana* of Safdarjung, 29th *Rabi* II 6th RY

Addressed to Zainul 'Abidin Khan. Whereas the *chaks* and (*muzra*) of village Barwaliya, *pargana* Salon the cultivated land had been previously resumed. To meet out the expenses of Shaikh Muhammad Ashraf and Shah Pir Ata, the revenues have been granted. Now some of the descendents of the former grantees are still interfering with the *chaks*, (this is illegal and unjustified) since these chaks were included in *khalisa* previously. Therefore, it is incumbent that the cultivated lands under grant are protected from previous grantees. In other respects also the grantees be provided all help.

Doc No. 11: Letter of Shuja Uddaulah to Shah Muhammad Panah, undated

Acknowledges the receipt of the gifts sent by mystic. Says that no orders has been issued to any of the *amils* for the resumption of the villages in his *aimma* grants. If any interference has been done inadvertantly, a *shuqqa* is being sent by hand to eliminate the chances of further interference. The addressee should not worry on this count.

Notes and References for the main text of the Chapter

1. Apart from the family manuscript, there are few biological notices of Shaikh Pir Muhammad in the 18th Century Chronical and *tazkirahs*. This is obviously because of the fact that his grandson, Saiyid Sadullah of Salon obtained greater prominance subsequently as a theologican and a sufi. In all his biographical noticies, he is referred to as the grandson of Shaikh Pir Muhammad who in turn is called the great mystic and theologican of his times. See Khafi Khan, *Muntakhab-ul-Lubab*, Bib. Indi. Kolkata, 1860-74, Vol. II, pp. 559-60; Ghulam Ali Azad Bilgirami, *Mathir-ul-Kiram*, Hyderabad, 1913, Vol. I p. 217. For independent, references to him see Muhammad Bukhtawar Khan, *Mirat-ul-Alam* (edited Dr. Sajida Alvi), Lahore, 1979 Vol. II, p. 417; Abdul Hai, *Nuzhat-ul-Khwatir*, Hyderabad, 1911, Vol. V, pp. 97-8.
2. The 19th century British officials and travellers trazversing southern Awadh, have left notices of the establishment. See Donald Butler, *Topography and Statistics of Southern Districts of Awadh*, Kolkata 1839, pp. 138-9 and 164-5 (Delhi Reprint 1982), WH Sleman, *Journey through the kingdom of Ovde in 1849-050* 2 vols. 1858, Vol. 1, pp. 232-4; *Gazetteer of the*

Province of Oudh, 3 vols, 1877, p. 290, HR Nevill, District Gazetteer of United Provinces (Rae Bareli), Allahabad 1923, Vol. 39, pp. 100-130, Beside to these printed works, there is a good deal of information in the files of Boorl of revenue, Allahabad (Now shifted to Allahabad) relating to the period of First Regular Settlement of Awadh in 1861.

3. The text of these *farman* could not be traced, but they have been discussed by WC Wood in his dispatch to the Commissioner of Baiswara Division in the course of his examining all the deeds of the grantees and their credentials to hold a number of villages in revenue free tenures. See letter no. 504 dated 13 July 1861 File Nos. 173 and 1870/1861-2 (Rae Bareli District) *Board of Revenue Lucknow*. (Hereafter as Wood's Dispatch).
4. Butler, *op. cit.,* pp. 138-9
5. *Ibid.*, p. 165.
6. Sleeman, *op. cit.*
7. I have not been able to examine the contents of the *sanad*, but an extract of it has been reproduced and discussed in a judicial decision of Allahabad High Court (Muhammad Shamsuddin Vs. Shah Muhammad Naeem Ata, *AIR* (1927), p. 7.
8. *Iqrarnamah* of Shah Karim 'Ata in favour of Shah Ashraf 'Ata dated 11th Zilhij 1238AH/1822 filed in Regular Suit No. 12 of 1880 decided on 14.2.1882, in the court of sub judge Rae Bareli Shah Muhammad Usman Ghani 'Ata' vs Muhammad Mehdi 'Ata and others.
9. Copy of this *iqrarnamah* is also filed in RS No. 12 of 1880 in the court of sub judge Rae Bareli decided on 14.2.1882.
10. Ghulam Ali Azad Bilgirami, *Mathir-ul Kiram*, Kanpur 1913, Vol. I, pp. 221-2.
11. See my unpublished thesis entitled 'Agrarian Conditions of Awadh under the Mughals and Nawab Wazirs, 1595-1856 submitted at AMU Aligarh, 1985, pp. 285-8
12. Ghulam Husain Khan, '*Imad-us Saadat*, Newalkishore, Lucknow, 1897, pp. 7-8.

13. Santosh Rae, *Insha-i Mansur* or *Mansure-ul Maktubat*, letters on behalf of Safdarjung addressed to Emperor Muhammad Shah and Wazir Qamaruddin Khan. these were collected by one Awadhi Lal in 212 AH/AD 1803. The only manuscript is preserved at Tagore Library, Lucknow University see pp. 46b-47a.

References for the Documents in Appendix

1. An early copy of the *farman* was in possession of Shah Muhammad Hussain Jafri, IXth Sajjadanashin of Khanqah Salon (1966-709). The contents of this documents has been described and translated by me in "Two madad-e-maash *farmans* of Aurangzeb from Awadh, PIHC (1979), pp. 302-14 pp. of this book. The document was destroyed during the course of unfortunate invidents at AMU on 13th May 1981. It was transcribed by Professor Irfan Habib for his use, and he has now kindly allowed me to reproduce the text in full.
2. Ibid.
3. The text of the letter is reproduced is a late family text, *Ashraf-ul Insha*; a collection of the letters exchanged between Shaikh Pir Muhammad and Shaikh Pir Muhammad Ashraf with his contemporary divines, princes and other notables, Ms. 1734, pp-24-3a (in the private collection of Shah Muhammad Jalil Ata, now residing at Karachi, who kindly allowed me to have the photocopy of the manuscript).
4. *Ibid.*
5. Photographic reproduction (obverse side) of this *farman* appears in Shah Muhammad Hasan Ata, *Harir-e Sang*, Nacees Academy, Karachi, 1963, p. 119.
6. The contents of this *farman* are described in W.C. Wood's dispatch, op. cit., 3-4. However, the transcript of this *farman* has been filed in Regular Suit No. 5 of 1945 in the court of sub-judge Partapgarh (Shah Muhammad Naeem 'Ata Sajadanasheen vs Sunni Central Board of waqfs v). The file of the said suit is now available at the Record Room of the Civil Court Rae Bareli (U.P.)

7. The documents is in private collection of Shah Muhammad Hameed 'Ata Hassan, now residing at Karachi, who kindly allowed me to have the photocopy of the document.
8. Ibid.
9. Ibid.
10. Ibid.
11. Ibid.

Appendix

I wish to acknowledge the kindness of my teacher Professor Ishtiyaq Ahmad Zilli for making the transcript of Document No. 1 and 2. He was kind enough to transcribe them in the legible fair hand from the extensive personal notes prepared by Professor Irfan Habib from these documents before they were destroyed in an unfortunate incident of arson of my hostel room during an ugly incident at Aligarh Muslim University Campus way back on 13th May 1981.

The rest 6 documents were kindly transcribed by my friend Mr. Syed Aslam Ali, Talab Mulla Eram, Rampur from my notes of these documents. I am most thankfull to him as well.

Documents from Khanqah-i-Karimia Pargana Salon

Document No. 8. Transcript of the *Farman* of Mughal emperor Aurangzeb (19th RY/ AD 1676) in favour of Hazrat Shaikh Pir Muhammad of Salon (d. 1687).

بسم الله الرحمن الرحیم

یا ایها الذین آمنوا اطیعوا الله و اطیعوا الرسول
و اولی الامر منکم

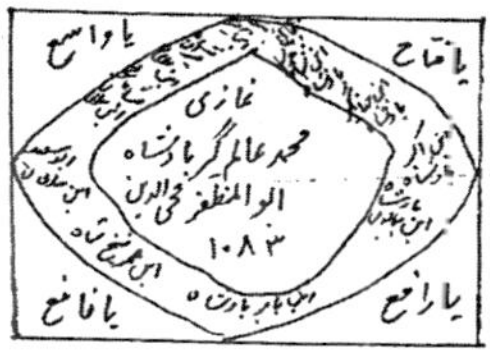

چون بعرض مقدس معلی رسید که بموجب اسناد حکام موازی دو صد بیگه زمین از موضع مرزا بختیارپور
معموله پرگنه نصیرآباد سرکار مانکپور مضاف صوبه الهآباد در وجه نذر خادمان حقائق و معارف آگاه شیخ پیر محمد
ساکن پرگنه سلون مقرر است و بر اراضی مزبوره قابض و متصرف اند امیدوار اند که در آن باب
فرمان والاشان مرحمت شود حکم جهان مطاع عالم مطیع صادر شد که زمین مسطور از محل قدیم بدستور سابق
بشرط قبض و تصرف در وجه مدد معاش آنها حسب الضمن مقرر باشد که حاصلات آن را
صرف مایحتاج خود می نموده بدعای بقای دولت روز افزون مواظبت نمایند باید که حکام و عمال
و جاگیرداران و کروریان حال و استقبال اراضی مذکوره بتصرف آنها بازگذارند و اصلاً و مطلقاً تغیر و تبدیل
بدان راه ندهند و بعلت مال و جهات و اخراجات مثل و قنلغه و پیشکش و جریبانه و ضابطانه و محصلانه
و مهرانه و داروغگانه و بیگار و شکار و مقدمی و قانونگوئی [و] ضبط هر ساله و تکرار زراعت و
کل تکالیف دیوانی و مطالبات سلطانی مزاحم نشوند و درین باب هر سال سند مجدد نه طلبند
اگر در محلی دیگر داشته باشند آنرا اعتبار نکنند پنجم شهر شوال سال نوزدهم (19) جلوس والا
نوشته شد.

سید علی موسوی قاضی خادم شرع مصطفوی ۱۲۱۲

مطابق اصل

شاه محمد حسین سجاده نشین سلون

شاه محمد حسین جعفری سجاده نشین خانقاه کریمیه سلون ۱۳۸۵ ہجری

شرح یادداشت واقعه تاریخ روز سه‌شنبه چهاردهم شهر رجب المرجب سنه ۱۹ جلوس والا موافق
سنه ۱۰۸۶ هجری مطابق امر قور ماه الهی برسالت سیادت ونقابت پناه شرافت ونجابت
دستگاه سزاوار رعایت بادشاهی قابل مرحمت شاهنشاهی صدر رفیع القدر رضویخان
ونوبت واقعه نویسی کمترین بنده درگاه خلایق پناه عنایت الله قلمی میگردد که حسب التماس
امارت وایالت پناه شهامت وبسالت دستگاه همت خان بعرض مقدس معلی رسید که
بموجب اسناد حکام موازی دوصد بیگه زمین از موضع مرزا بختیار [پور] عمله پرگنه نصیرآباد
سرکار مانکپور مضاف بصوبه اله آباد در وجه نذر خادمان حقایق ومعارف آگاه شیخ میر محمد
امیدوار اند که درین باب فرمان والاشان مرحمت شود حکم جهان مطاع عالم مطیع صادر که اراضی
مسطور از محلقدیم بدستور سابق بشرط قبض وتصرف در وجه مدد معاش آنها مرحمت فرمودیم اگر
در محل دیگر چیزی داشته باشند آنرا اعتبار نکنند واقعه ۵ رجب سنه ۱۸ بموجب تصدیق یادداشت
قلمی شد شرح مؤتمن الدوله العلیه معتمد السلطنة البهیه عمده وزرای رفیع الشان
زبده خوانین بلند مکان شایسته انواع عنایت سزاوار اصناف مرحمت خان سعادت
نشان جمدة الملک مدار المهام اسد خان که [آنکه] داخل واقعه نمایند شرح بخط سیادت
ونقابت پناه شرافت ونجابت دستگاه صدر رفیع القدر رضویخان که [آنکه] داخل واقعه
نمایند شرح بخط واقعه نویس مطابق واقعه است شرح بخط عمده وزرای رفیع الشان زبدة الخوانین
بلند مکان خان شجاعت نشان جمدة الملک مدار المهام که [آنکه] بعرض مکرر رسانند شرح بخط
فضائل پناه کمالات دستگاه شیخ عبد العزیز آنکه یازدهم رمضان سنه ۱۹ جلوس مبارک مکرر
بعرض مقدس رسید شرح بخط لایق العنایت والاحسان بهره مند خان بنیابت خان
خان شجاعت نشان جمدة الملک که [آنکه] فرمان عالیشان قلمی نمایند تسبیحه

۲۰۰ بیگه زمین از محلقدیم بدستور سابق

بموجب یادداشت واقعه فرمان والاشان قلمی شد

بمعرفت خان محمد قلمی شد

داخل نموده

بتاریخ ۱۲ ذی قعده سنه ۱۹ جلوس والا

نوبت [؟] بدفتر دیوان صدارت بمعرفت خان محمد رسید

بواقعه مقابله شد

داخل روزنامچه واقعه ۱۴ ذی قعده سنه ۱۹ داخل ...

داخل اوارجه
بتاریخ ۹ شهر ذی الحجه سنه ۱۹ جلوس والا موافق سنه ۱۰۸۶ هجری نقل بدفتر المر رسید بمعرفت خان محمد
تاریخ شهر ذی حجه سنه ۱۹ جلوس والا نقل بدفتر توجیه تفصیل [؟] رسید بمعرفت خان محمد
برسالت سیادت ونقابت پناه شرافت ونجابت دستگاه سزاوار عنایت بادشاهی قابل مرحمت
خلیفه الهی صدر رفیع القدر رضویخان ونوبت واقعه نویسی عنایت الله تسبیحه

Document No. 9. Transcript of the *Farman* of Mughal emperor Aurangzeb (22nd RY/ AD 1629) in favour of Hazrat Shah Pir Muhammad Ashraf of Salon (d. 1754).

بسم الله الرحمن الرحیم

یا ایها الذین آمنوا اطیعوا الله و اطیعوا الرسول و اولی الامر منکم

یا فتاح یا دامح

عالمگیر بادشاه غازی

محمد محی الدین

ابوالمظفر ۱۰۸۲

یا رافع یا ناسخ

نقل

فرمان واجب الاذعان بمهر ابوالمظفر محی الدین حضرت محمد عالمگیر بادشاه غازی بنام
شاه پیر محمد اشرف سلونی آنکه در نیوشت فرمان والاشان صادر شد که موضع
سنکهول در بست من اعمال و پرگنه سلون تابع سرکار مانکپور مضاف صوبه الهآباد
که سی و دو هزار و یکصد دام جمع آنست از نصف ربیع خوی ییل در وجه مدد معاش
شیخ محمد اشرف ولد شیخ پیر محمد حسب الضمن مقرر باشد که محاصلات آن را صرف
معیشت خود نموده بدعاء بقاء دولت ابد طراز اشتغال نماید باید که حکام و متصدیان و
[عمّال] حال و استقبال موضع مذکور را متصرف او باز گزارند و از جمیع وجوه و عوارض معاف
و مرفوع القلم شناسند [و درین] باب هر ساله سند مجدد نطلبند اگر در محلے دیگر جزے داشته باشند
آنرا اعتبار نکنند شانزدهم جمادی الاولی سال بست و دوم از جلوس والا نوشته شد.

قاضی سید شرف [؟] علی رضوی ولد سید عطا علی رضوی خادم شرع ۱۲۳۱

مطابق اصل

شاه محمد حسین جعفری سجاده نشین خانقاه .

شرح یادداشت واقعه بتاریخ روز چهارشنبه بیست و یکم شهر ربیع الاول سنه ۲۲ جلوس والا موافق ۱۳۸۵
سنه ۱۰۹۰ هجری مطابق ماه الهی بر ساله سیادت و نقابت پناه شرافت و نجابت دستگاه

سزاوار عنایت پادشاهی قابل مرحمت شاهنشاهی صدر رفیع القدر رضوی خان و لوبت واقعه نویسی کمترین بندگان
درگاه خلائق پناه دولتمند قلمی میگردد که از روی نوشته میر محمد مهاکردی واقعه نگار صوبه اوده بعرض
والا رسید که شیخ محمد اشرف پسر حقائق آگاه شیخ پیر محمد ساکن پرگنه سلون سرکار مانکپور تابع صوبه الهآباد
که بکمال آراستگی دارد بر خاندی زمینداران در موضع سنگهول معموله پرگنه مذکور متوطن گرفته آنرا
اشرف آباد نام نهاده و سید عبد الرحیم صدر جزو الهآباد نیز تجویز نامه داده امیدوار است که سند درگاه
مرحمت شود حکم جهانمطاع عالم مطیع صادر شد که موضع مذکور نسلاً بعد نسل ابداً مؤبداً در لبست
در وجه مدد معاش او مرحمت فرموده‌ایم و اگر در محلی دیگر چیزی داشته باشد آنرا اعتبار نکنند . . .
واقعه ۲۶ ذی قعده سنه ۲۲ مطابق تصدیق . . . یادداشت قلمی شد شرح بخط مؤتمن الدوله العالیه
معتمد السلطنة السنیه [؟] عمده وزرای رفیع الشان زبده خوانین بلند مکان شایسته انواع
عنایت سزاوار اضعاف مرحمت خان شجاعت نشان جملة الملک مدار المهام اسد خان آنکه داخل
[واقعه نمایند] ولقابت پناه . . . دستگاه صدر رفیع القدر رضوی خان آنکه داخل واقعه نمایند شرح
بخط واقعه نویس مطابق واقعه است شرح بخط شایسته انواع عنایت سزاوار اضعاف مرحمت
خان شجاعت نشان جملة الملک مدار المهام آنکه بعرض مکرر رسانند شرح بخط خانه زاد سزاوار عنایت
والاحسان لایق المرحمة والامتنان لطف الله خان آنکه دوازدهم ربیع الثانی سنه ۲۲ جلوس میمنت مانوس
مکرر بعرض مقدس رسید شرح بخط خان شجاعت نشان جملة الملک مدار المهام آنکه فرمان عالیشان
قلمی نمایند

شرح بخط جملة الملک مدار المهام آنکه [؟] بنظر درآمد

شرح سیاهه یکموضع در لبست مقرراً

مقرراً شخواه موضع سنگهول عمله پرگنه سلون سرکار مانکپور صوبه الهآباد

المالیه

[؟] وغیره

مقررا [؟] بقرار سراسری در لبست

موضع در لبست

Document No. 10. The Undated letter of Mughal emperor Aurangzeb addressed to Hazrat Shaikh Pir Muhammad of Salon, inviting him to visit Delhi.

سالک مسالک طریقت واقف موافق حقیقت زاد عرفانه

بعد اهداء سلام مسنون خلاصة المرام اینکه در این وقت همت والا نهمت

مصروف به استیصال فجره دکن است. رسیدن مابدولت اقبال برای

ملاقات ان زبدة العارفین متعسر است اگر خود برای زیارت پیران خود

که در دهلی اسوده اند تشریف آرند استفاده برکات از ملاقات ان ملکی

صفات کرده آید والسلام.

Document No. 11. Reply of Hazrat Shaikh Pir Muhammad of Salon to the letter of invitation from the emperor, politely refusing to visit Delhi.

شاهان دین پناه، فقیر را این حوصله نمانده، این دهقانی را با بزم

سلطانی چه کار گاهی گاهی کسی از راهی می آید در کریم باز است و کریم ما

بی نیاز است، کریمی دارم که چون گرسنه می شوم مهمانی می کند و چون

می خسپم پاسبانی می کند و چون گناه می کنم مهربانی، کریم ما بس باقی هوس.

Document No. 12. Transcript of the copy of a letter from Hazrat Shah Pir Ashraf to the first Nawab of Awadh, Nawab Burhanul Mulk Saadat Ali Khan (d. 1739) with the endorsement of the Nawab on the top left of the same sheet. This is regarding the restoration of his resume *aimma* villages by the officials of the Nawab.

قاضی سید لطیف
خادم شرع محمدی

کما اصله

شرح دستخط آنکه شده... بتوجهات حضرات
ایمه اطهار وفقراء وصحابه اهل اسلام شد قلع وقمع
این کا کشته باعث تقویت دین محمدی صلی الله علیه واله
شد حقائق ومعارف آگاه درین باب دیهات خود که نوشته اند
پروانه به اسمی نوشته فرستاده والسلام.

نقل خط پیر شاه محمد اشرف صاحب بدستخط خاص نواب برهان الملک

آنکه نواب صاحب السیف والقلم بنوا... دان عالم سلامت که بهره رابطه
اتحاد جلسه است چه مجال قلمرانی که نا محرم ازینمعنی بنابر عنان شبدیز
قلم را رهگرای قضای مدعائے سازد که روز شب از صدق اخلاص صمیمی ترقی
عمر و دولت از درسامع الدعوات مسالت مینماید الهی سالهاے سال و قرنهاے
بے شمار ظل عالی وسایه متعالی برتارک عالم وعالمیان تا الیوم القیام قائم دارد آمین.
دیگر آنکه درینولا استماع جنگ مقهور که بسزای کردار خود رسید وفتح وفیروزی نصیب
نواب صاحب کردند مبارکها باد هزاران سجده شکر بدرگاه رب العزت می آورده
که از نزول دائره عالی بالضلع دین اسلام قایم گردید ازدی دانیکه حکم عالی
برضبطی ایمه صوبجات گردیده همه جا سوار و پیاده عاملان سرکار نشسته اند.
بر دیهات اینجانب هم آمده اند باوجودیکه پروانه عالی متعالی کل دیهات
اینجانب حاصل است گماشته مرشد قلی خان پروانه اسمی میخواهند بنابر عرض
نموده آید که لطف قدیم مرعی داشته پروانه باسم مرزا معز الیه صادر گردد
که از جمله و دیهات محمد اشرف مزاحم نشوند درینصورت خرج خانقاه
و فقراء بحال می باید. [رساله سوه مم الزه؟]

Document No. 13. Copy of the undated *Parwana* of the second Nawab of Awadh, Nawab Abul Mansur Safdarjung (d. 1754) to his official namely Zainul Abididn Khan for excluding the *aimma* villages of Shah Muhammad Ashraf from the general order of the resumption.

النقل مطابق له

خادم شرع نبوی سید عطا علی قاضی رضوی ۱۱۷۸

نقل پروانه نواب ابوالمنصور خان بهادر مرقوم ۲۹ ربیع الثانی سنه ۶ جلوس والا آنکه رفعت
و عوالی پناه زین العابدین خان در حفظ الهی باشند موضع بردلیا عمله پرگنه سلون چون مزرعه ها
و چکوک سابق واقع موضع مذکور که در عمل ضبطی بودند در وجه خرج فقرائی قدوة العارفین
شاه پیر محمد اشرف صاحب و شاه پیر عطا صاحب از حضور معاف و مشخص منها است
درینولا اکثری از اولاد ائمه داران در چکوک مذکوره مداخلت خلاف معمول میخواهد
هرگاه که پیش از عمل سرکار چکوک مسطوره بعمل ضبطی در آمد حکم خالصه داشت .
دعوی آنها نامسموع است لهذا نگارش میرود که آنها را ازین امر باز دارند
و دیهه را معه چکوک درست موافق معمول فقراء معاف شناسند و دوباره
محتاج تاکید حضور نشود در هر امور ممد و معاون فقرا باشند درینباب
قدغن بلیغ دانند .

Document No. 14. Copy of the undated letter of the third Nawab of Awadh, Nawab Shujauddaula (d. 1774) to Shah [Muhammad Panah, died 1785] assuring him that a separate *parwana* is being sent to the concerned officials for the restorations of his resumed *aimma* villages.

کما اصلہ

بنوی
خادم شرع
سید عطا علی
قاضی رضوی

نقل خط بمہر نواب شجاع الدولہ بہادر

آنکہ حقائق و معارف آگاہ زبدۃ السالکین قدوۃ العارفین شاہ صاحب سلمہ اللہ تعالی

الطاف نامہ معہ چیترہا منعقش ناد علی و شیرین تبرک رسیدہ مسرور ساخت

و از توجہ باطنی کہ بدعائے خیر زیادہ می دارند کمال شفقت پنداشت آئندہ

ہم در حین مکاشفۂ محمدیت با ادعیۂ ماثورہ مذکور باید داشت آنچہ

در باب دیہات آئمہ رفتہ بود از سرکار برائے ضبطی دیہات ان حقائق

آگاہ ہرگز بکس عامل قلمی نشدہ سہواً ۔۔ تعرض دارند شقہ بمہر دستی می رسد

چہ امکان کہ احدی مزاحمت تواند گردید ازین ممر خاطر شریف مطمئن

فرمایند والسلام ۔

Document No. 15. *Farman* of Awadh King Nasiruddin Hydar (d. 1837) issued in recognition of the *tauliyat* of Shah Panah Ata (d. 1860) over the *waqf* properties of the *khanqah* situated in the *parganahs* of Salon, Pershadepur, Jais, Manikpur and Behar. It also goes on to say that after his death, his son and successor Shah Husain Ata (d. 1880) shall act as a new *mutawalli*.

مسرت ظل سبحانی سلیما نجاه خلد الله ملکه و اله
نقل مهر بادشاهی
ابو النصر --- سلیما نجاه
سلطان --- نصیر الدین حیدر غازی بادشاه

بمهر بیضوی دستخط خاص کرامت اختصاص بنام مولوی شاه محمد
پناه عطا ابن و ے سجاده نشین شاه کریم عطا سلونی رحمة الله علیه مرقوم
بست و هفتم رجب سنه ۱۲۵۱ هجری متصدیان مهمات حال و استقبال سلون
وغیره بدانند قدوة العرفا شاه پیر کریم عطا سلونی در سه فرزند صلبی
خود .... پیر محمد پناه عطا را سجاده نشین و قائم مقام ذات خود
گردانیده بر درگاه سابق و جمع املاک و ملک قابض و متصرف
نموده استدعاء منظوری تولیت و سجاده نشینی بحضور اقدس
اعلیٰ نموده .... ست منظور فرموده دیهات و چکوک و باغات
و عمارات که در جاگیر سلون و پرشدپور و جائیس و مانکپور و بهار
وغیره که از قدیم الایام برائی اعراس ائمه اطهار و مصارف سجاده
نشین صادر خانقاه و مساجد معاف و از دفتر حشو و منهاء است
الحال بنام مولوی شاه پیر محمد پناه عطا و سجاده نشین او مولوی
شاه محمد حسین عطا بلا شرکت و سهامت بدستور قدیم نسلاً بعد نسلٍ و بطناً بعد بطنٍ
موبداً معاف و قلم داشته شد باید که ناظمان و جاگیرداران و متصدیان حال و استقبال پرگنات
از استقلال و استمرار این حکم اقدس کوشیده حاصلات آنرا تصرف مولوی مذکور بوجهی من الوجوه
از بهنت و بیگار و جریبانه و نذرانه وغیره ابواب فوجداری و تحصیلداری پته داری تعرض مزاحمت
نرسانند و هرگونه ممد و معاون صاحب سجاده بوده مملوکه سجاده نشین، دیگر برادر شریک و سهیم
نسازند که ناظمان بخاطر بیاد الهی موظف و بدعای دولت ابد مدت اشتغال
باشند درینباب تاکید مزید شناخته هر سال سند مجدد نطلبند فقط.

Index

C

D

E

F

K

L

M

N

O

P

Q

R

S

Y

Z